D0053756

1,000*

unforgettable

SENIOR
MOMENTS

{ *Of Which We Could*
Remember Only 254 }

UPDATED SECOND EDITION

1,000*
unforgettable
SENIOR
MOMENTS

by TOM . . . uh . . . FRIEDMAN

{ *Of Which We Could
Remember Only 254 }

WORKMAN PUBLISHING • NEW YORK

"Memory is the thing you forget with."
—Alexander Chase, *Perspectives*

Copyright © 2006, 2017 by Tom Friedman

All rights reserved. No portion of this book may be reproduced—mechanically, electronically, or by any other means, including photocopying—without written permission of the publisher. Published simultaneously in Canada by Thomas Allen & Son Limited.

Library of Congress Cataloging-in-Publication Data is available.

ISBN 978-0-7611-9367-8

Design by Paul Hanson and Galen Smith

Author photo by Christy M. Newman

Workman books are available at special discounts when purchased in bulk for premiums and sales promotions as well as for fund-raising or educational use. Special editions or book excerpts can also be created to specification. For details, contact the Special Sales Director at the address below, or send an email to specialmarkets@workman.com.

Workman Publishing Co., Inc.
225 Varick Street
New York, NY 10014-4381
workman.com

WORKMAN is a registered trademark of
Workman Publishing Co., Inc.

Printed in China
First printing May 2017

10 9 8 7 6 5 4 3 2

To Christy, Corey, and Jonathan

INTRODUCTION

It's been ten years since the first edition of *1,000* Unforgettable Senior Moments *Of Which We Could Remember Only 246* was published, and its success since then has surprised everyone—except, that is, for me, although I can't quite remember why. But no matter. Since that time, a new crop of absentminded folks has drifted past the point of denial to join the rest of us. So we've created a second edition. Really, what better way to celebrate this sobering rite of passage than a truly funny and reassuring book filled with historical anecdotes about the memory lapses of the rich, famous, and wonderfully eccentric?

If you're just joining the club, take comfort. You are not alone—not by a long shot.

Those of you who already have read the first edition may be wondering, why should you bother with a second one? Well, first, there are dozens of new anecdotes to chuckle over. And second, you've surely forgotten the classic ones we've kept and updated, and now you can enjoy them all over again.

Above all, this is the perfect book for anyone who is unable to conjure up the first or last name of the person who just came up and said, "It's so great to see you again!"

It's the book that's small enough to carry with you at all times so that you can open it at any page and see that countless others have experienced major mental lapses that make your own . . . well, hardly worth remembering.

If you're in your sixties, as I am, the first thing you may want to know about senior moments is: Are they really senior? I'm often asked this, and although I can't recall what I've said, I do have my notes, which suggest that the answer is yes, no, and maybe.

This is the perfect book for anyone who is unable to conjure up the first or last name of the person who just came up and said, "It's so great to see you again!"

The most familiar type of forgetting is absentmindedness, in which information is never properly encoded in your memory, if it's encoded at all. Consider this: If you learn a new piece of information (say, that the average blue whale can grow up to 100 feet long, weigh as much as 200 tons, and eat upward of 4 tons of krill a day if it's especially hungry), but you don't have a reason to use it soon afterward and imprint it in your memory, it may never stick.

As you grow older, you tend to remember the more important stuff and don't bother as much as you used to with the rest (unless, of course, you know a blue whale personally). That's why I like to think of senior moments as evidence of having a more discriminating mind. (You can try out this excuse the next time your loved ones get exasperated with you.)

But these lapses in memory can also be "junior moments" as well as senior ones. After all, teenagers can lose one jacket after another, making their parents crazy. They can study all week for a test and then forget what they studied and fail miserably.

But it *is* true that as we get older, we do seem to suffer bouts of forgetfulness more often. Certainly we're more conscious of our forgetfulness as we age, whereas kids tend to shrug it off.

There are also enormous differences among individuals in their ability to remember information, no matter their age. A 70-year-old can have a better memory than an 18-year-old. When my grandmother was 94, she could recall every student she taught in a Hungarian high school seventy-five years before, while I could not remember where I parked my car. West 88th Street in Manhattan? Boston? Budapest?

So getting older doesn't necessarily mean forgetting everything. That's the good news. But here, alas, is the bad news: There is another type of forgetting called "transience," which does occur more often as the years pass by. A number of studies have shown that seniors in general have more difficulty remembering information that they've been asked to learn than college students do. Even when older people recall information as well as younger folks, their memories fade

> I like to think of senior moments as evidence of having a more discriminating mind.

faster. And they also have more trouble remembering the precise details of something, even when they still recall the gist of it.

There's another variant of forgetting that can be age-related as well. It occurs when something has been stored in your memory but you can't retrieve it when you want to. For some of us, this is the most diabolical senior moment of all—the information that's on "the tip of your tongue." Scientists, who generally are an un-poetic lot, call this "blocking," and sadly, it happens more often among older people than younger ones; more often among 40-year-olds than 20-year-olds; and more often among 70-year-olds than 40-year-olds. These senior moments really *are* senior.

But if, after learning this, you're tempted to devote a great deal of time, energy, and money to trying to improve your memory significantly as you age, may I recommend my own approach, which is far easier and cheaper? Just mumble "It's so nice to see you" when cornered by someone whose name you can't recall, and avoid at all costs playing Trivial Pursuit, chess, and poker.

Look at it this way: If you can't recall what

keys are for, you have a big problem and need professional help right away. But if you simply can't remember where you placed them, you might as well laugh it off, which is what I try to do.

This book will definitely help you laugh it off. And here's the best part: You can read it over and over again and it will seem as fresh and funny as the day you bought it.

Embrace your senior moments! Just don't try to remember them.

—T. F.

WAIT, WAIT, HOW ABOUT
THE SUPREME COURT?

Texas Governor Rick Perry, on a quest for the 2012 Republican Party presidential nomination, had a senior moment setback in a televised debate while millions of people watched. When he set out to name three federal agencies he had pledged to eliminate if he were in the White House, he was able to come up with only two: the Commerce and Education departments, completely forgetting the Department of Energy. Finally, after straining to remember, he gave up with a simple and somewhat poignant "Oops." How fitting, then, that just four years later, in 2016, Perry was tapped by Donald Trump to guide the nation's energy policy as head of what the Texan once reviled and sought to destroy: the "Department That Cannot Be Recalled."

HEY, IT COULD HAVE BEEN FOR ASTROPHYSICS

Singer Nicki Minaj was a winner at the 2015 BET (Black Entertainment Television) Awards, but for what, exactly? Accepting the Viewers' Choice Award, she seemed to begin her acceptance speech, trophy in hand, but then stopped suddenly. "I'm sorry," she said. "What was this award for?"

EXERCISE? FORGET IT

In her nineties and still going strong, actress Betty White spoke in 2010 of the ultimate senior moments exercise regimen that was keeping her fit: "I have a two-story house and a bad memory," she explained. "I'm up and down those stairs all the time [asking], 'What did I come up here for again?'"

MAYBE THE ALIENS WERE
IN THE OVEN

Astronomers using Australia's most famous radio telescope believed they may well have discovered evidence of alien life when they picked up a distinctive signal at the same time every day. It was only seventeen years later, in 2015, that they remembered to check a civilization a lot closer to home. The signal was coming from a microwave oven used by staff members to heat up their lunches.

CERTAINLY NOT LIKE
THOSE HEATHENS

In the early 1950s, during a debate on the Middle East problem, Warren Austin, an American diplomat and U.S. delegate to the United Nations, sternly advised Jews and Arabs to "sit down and settle their differences like Christians."

WE DIDN'T PLAN ON
CHANGING CLOTHES, ANYWAY

In 2015, two Americans in their seventies decided to sail their yacht, *Nora*, across the Atlantic from Norway to the United States. Unfortunately, they had to be rescued nine times before they even left Europe. The men insisted that they were perfectly competent and merely the victims of bad luck. But one particular mishap, in Cornwall, England, came not while they were sailing but while they were tied up in the harbor. It seems they absentmindedly left a candle burning in the yacht when they went ashore to pick up some groceries. It fell over, as candles in boats tend to do, and set their spare clothes on fire.

BUT THOSE STATES ARE NEXT TO
EACH OTHER, RIGHT?

When Donald Trump spoke disparagingly of Hillary Clinton's running mate, he must have forgotten everything he learned in fifth-grade geography. He insisted in a televised speech, "Her running mate, Tim Kaine, who by the way did a terrible job in New Jersey. . . . He was not very popular in New Jersey, and he still isn't." Kaine, however, was the highly popular governor of *Virginia*, not New Jersey. It was Chris Christie, a fervent backer of Donald Trump, who was the (not very popular) governor of New Jersey.

BREAKING NEWS THAT'S ALREADY BROKEN!

There's nothing like senior moments that are broadcast live by an absentminded production staff. Here are just some of the alerts that news departments have put at the bottom of our TV screens: "Space Shuttle traveling nearly 18 times the speed of light!" (CNN); "Memorial Day Weekend: Buckle Up, Slow Down & Drink & Drive" (KARE 11, Minneapolis–St. Paul); and our personal favorite, "Fire destroyed by home" (Fox 5, Las Vegas).

NEXT YOU'LL BE ASKING ME TO PAY FOR THE LAST SUPPER!

When director Franco Zeffirelli explained that the high cost of the television miniseries *Jesus of Nazareth* was due in part to the salaries of the twelve actors who were hired to play the twelve apostles, producer Sir Lew Grade experienced a severe memory glitch. "Twelve? Who needs twelve?" he thundered. "Couldn't we make do with six?"

SU CASA ES MI CASA

Columbia University philosopher Irwin Edman once visited the home of a colleague. At 2 a.m. Edman's colleague began to yawn pointedly. When Edman didn't take the hint, the man said, "Irwin, I hate to put you out, but I have a nine o'clock class tomorrow morning." "Good Lord!" Irwin replied, "I thought you were in *my* house!"

WAIT, I CHANGED MY MIND—
MAKE THAT GRUEL

The Marquis de Condorcet had what seemed to be a good idea for escaping the Reign of Terror during the French Revolution. He dressed up as a peasant in ragged clothes and took off. Just before he reached the French border, he stopped at an inn full of hungry locals and, completely forgetting his disguise, ordered an extravagant omelet made with a dozen eggs. Instead of enjoying his meal, he was dragged away to prison.

BEATS "HEY, YOU!"

Because he couldn't remember anyone's name, Chuck Berry called everyone Jack. Zsa Zsa Gabor, who was once asked about her equally bad memory, replied, "Dahling, how do you think the 'dahling' thing got started?"

THE FIRST ANNUAL G. K. CHESTERTON AWARD FOR ABSENTMINDEDNESS GOES TO . . . G. K. CHESTERTON!

The notoriously absentminded and disorganized British writer G. K. Chesterton was devoted to his mother. When he became engaged, he shared the happy news by writing a long letter to her. It would have been an even more thoughtful gesture had his mother not already been sitting in the same room when he wrote it.

WELL AT LEAST IT COOLED HIM OFF

During the 2002 Formula One season, racecar driver Pedro de la Rosa was far from happy. His modified Jaguar was too slow, difficult to drive, and always breaking down. But it was the United States Grand Prix race in Indianapolis that truly did him in. After lagging behind the field, his car caught fire, forcing the incensed driver to jump out. A track official then rushed over and told de la Rosa to hop over a small wall to ensure his safety as other cars zoomed by. Still fuming over his car's performance, de la Rosa angrily complied, only to discover that the race marshal had forgotten to mention one tiny detail. On the other side of the wall was a small river, into which de la Rosa promptly fell.

BETTER YET, HAVE HIM CALL ME

One evening the German dramatist and philosopher Gotthold Ephraim Lessing, who was completely lost in thought, realized he had forgotten his house key. When he knocked on his front door, a servant looked out the window and, not recognizing Lessing in the dark, called out, "The professor is not at home," to which Lessing replied, "Oh, very well. No matter." He then turned around and started walking away, saying: "Tell him I'll call another time."

COMING NEXT: HOW TO HOTWIRE A CAR WHEN YOU LOSE YOUR KEYS

When politicians have senior moments, it usually goes badly. Certainly that was the case with Oakland, California, Mayor Jean Quan. It must have slipped her mind that a city plagued by burglaries might be sensitive about anything that would improve the skills of would-be criminals. In 2013, her online newsletter promoted a class on how to pick locks. The explanation that the class was intended for people who absentmindedly misplaced their keys did not sit too well with voters. The class was canceled, and Mayor Quan lost the next election.

OBJECTION FORGOTTEN!

Throughout the nation, a plague of senior moments has infiltrated our court system for years. Here's just one excerpt from an actual court transcript. LAWYER: "This myasthenia gravis, does it affect your memory at all?" WITNESS: "Yes." LAWYER: "And in what way does it affect your memory?" WITNESS: "I forget." LAWYER: "You forget? Can you give us an example of something you've forgotten?"

BUT HE DID REMEMBER IT WAS LONDON

In October 1944, Welsh poet Dylan Thomas failed to appear at his friend Vernon Watkins's London wedding, at which Thomas was scheduled to serve as best man. After the ceremony, Watkins received an envelope from Thomas. It contained two letters. The first one apologized for having forgotten the name of the church. The second one apologized for having forgotten to mail the first letter.

ALTHOUGH NOT AS GREAT
AS IT COULD HAVE BEEN

When Richard Nixon arrived in Paris for the funeral of French President Georges Pompidou in April 1974, his mind must have been elsewhere. At the airport he declared, "This is a great day for France!"

AND PLEASE GIVE MY REGARDS
TO HIS LOVELY WIFE

Sir Thomas Beecham, who in 1932 founded the London Philharmonic Orchestra, once ran into a distinguished looking woman in the lobby of a hotel. Although he could not remember her name, he thought he knew her. When he engaged her in conversation, he vaguely recollected that she had a brother. Hoping for any clue as to her identity, he asked her how her brother was and whether he was still working at the same job. "Oh, he's very well," said Princess Mary about George VI, "and still king."

YOU MEAN SHE WASN'T A PHANTOM?

In 2009, German authorities were desperately trying to find the "phantom of Heilbronn," a woman thought to have murdered six people over sixteen years, including a police officer in the city of Heilbronn. Traces of her DNA were found at forty different crime scenes in three countries. But because the DNA wasn't in any national or international database, her identity remained unknown. A puzzle suitable for Sherlock Holmes? Not exactly. Detectives in Germany, Austria, and France hadn't stopped to consider alternative theories to that of a wandering killer. As it turned out, the cotton swabs used to collect all the samples had been contaminated. And the "diabolical culprit" was an absentminded 71-year-old medical worker who handled the swabs before sending them off to police labs in the places where the crimes were committed.

WE WANTED THAT FRESH, OPEN LOOK

A new jail in Jacksonville, Florida, was about to open to great fanfare in 1995. It cost $35 million to build and was everything a community could want in a prison—except for one minor problem: County officials forgot to order doors for the 195 cells.

AND IT'S ENTIRELY POSSIBLE
I HAD PARENTS, TOO

D rew Barrymore was asked by *Premiere* magazine in 2001 whether she hoped to have children. "Definitely!" she said. "I would like to have at least two, because

I didn't have a brother or sister growing up." Suddenly she paused. "I mean, I *have* a brother, but we didn't really spend a lot of time together." Again, she stopped. "And I have a sister, too."

THAT'S OKAY, HE WOULDN'T HAVE FOUND A RAZOR ANYWAY

A friend of Ludwig van Beethoven's named Frederick Stark called on him one morning and found the great but forgetful composer in his bedroom, getting dressed. Curiously, Beethoven's face was covered with a thick layer of dried soap. He had lathered his face the night before, planning to shave, then forgotten to do so and gone to bed.

OH, I THOUGHT MOZART GOT IT FROM ME

Once, while in London, singer-songwriter Neil Diamond heard some familiar music and mentioned it was from his hit "Song Sung Blue." His companion quickly corrected him, saying, "No, they're playing Mozart." "Oh," said Diamond, who had conveniently forgotten he borrowed the music from Mozart's Piano Concerto No. 21.

BEWARE THE WRATH OF GOOGLE

Lindsay Diaz's house in Rowlett, Texas, managed to survive a ferocious tornado in 2015. But while her home could withstand the fury of nature, it couldn't survive the power of an app. Instead of directing a demolition crew to the right place—a condemned duplex a block away—Google Maps led them to Diaz's front door. Forgetting to recheck the address, the crew members proceeded to turn her house into rubble. Then, not wanting to waste valuable time apologizing, they doubled back and tore down the condemned duplex.

LET'S HAVE HIM OVER FOR DINNER AS SOON AS POSSIBLE

The names of friends and acquaintances often escaped the mind of playwright Howard Lindsay (one of the authors of the stage version of *The Sound of Music*). Sometimes this had unexpected

consequences, as when he was engaged in
a long, bitter feud with a particular actor.
For years he refused to stay in the same
room with him when they accidentally
met, but one evening Lindsay's wife was
astonished to find her husband engaged in
a warm conversation with his nemesis at a
Hollywood dinner party. The conversation
ended with a burst of laughter, and after
Lindsay slapped the actor on the back, he
came over to his wife and whispered in her
ear, "Who was that fellow I was just talking
to, anyhow?"

WHERE WAS THE INVISIBLE HAND
WHEN HE NEEDED IT?

Adam Smith, the founding father of
modern economics and the author
of *The Wealth of Nations*, was notoriously
absentminded. He once put bread and
butter into a teapot and, after tasting the
result, declared it to be the worst cup of
tea he had ever had.

JUST DON'T SIT TOO CLOSE
TO THE HEAD

Members of the Georgia State Game Commission were going back and forth considering the merits of an item on their agenda: the regulation of alligator rides. There were some testy exchanges before one alert official—obviously the only alert one in the room—realized that thanks to an assistant's typo, they were discussing a nonexistent recreation instead of the real agenda item: a discussion about regulating the sale of alligator *hides*.

NEXT YEAR LET'S ASSIGN HIM
TO THE POLE VAULT

It was the 1932 Olympics, and competitors in the 3,000-meter race were coming around the bend for the final lap. Unfortunately, an official was gazing in the wrong direction and therefore neglected to ring the bell to signal the last lap. After the athletes crossed what should have been

the finish line, they just kept on running.
The favorite to win, a Finn named Volmari
Iso-Hollo, wound up first, but because he
ran an extra 450 meters before the official
snapped out of his senior moment, he
registered the slowest-ever time for the
3,000.

THIS SURE IS ONE SATISFYING BILDUNGSROMAN

The Russian critic and philosopher
Mikhail Bakhtin was working on a
major new work about the "bildungsroman"
genre (a bildungsroman is a coming-of-age
novel of spiritual, moral, or psychological
development). Working furiously to finish it,
Bakhtin, a heavy smoker, suddenly found
himself without any rolling paper to make
cigarettes, an intolerable situation. Not
having money to spare, he absentmindedly
looked around his room for a substitute
and grabbed the first thing at hand, thus
managing, over the next couple of hours, to
smoke away several drafts of his manuscript.

NO, NO, NOT THE OTTOMAN!

For a scene she was shooting for the classic movie *Some Like It Hot*, Marilyn Monroe was supposed to enter a room, walk to a dresser, rummage through the drawers, find a bottle of bourbon, and ask for a drink. She blew the line fifty-two times in a row—although far from her earlier record of

eighty-two takes. "On the fifty-third take," recalled director Billy Wilder, "I told her we had put the line on pieces of paper, and they were in every drawer she would open." However, added Wilder, "she went to the wrong piece of furniture."

I'LL TAKE THE FORTIES, TOO, IF YOU GOT 'EM

An out-of-work shoe salesman, who was trying to make ends meet, decided to rob a bank in Queens, New York. The beginning of the note he handed to the teller demonstrated a keen recall of U.S. currency denominations: "Give me all your tens, twenties . . . ," it began. But then his memory failed him: ". . . and thirties," the note concluded.

FURTHERMORE, WE SHALL FIGHT THEM ON THE BEACHES!

The Baroness Trumpington of Sandwich stood up and began addressing the House of Lords about the wages paid to babysitters and nannies. "There has been much confusion on this matter," she declared, more accurately than she knew. After five minutes of an increasingly heated speech, she suddenly stopped and said, "My lords, I have been speaking on the wrong subject." Members of the House had been debating an amendment to a social security bill when the baroness took the floor and began reading from the wrong notes.

AND THE ONE ABOUT
"FOUR SCORE AND SEVEN YEARS
AGO"—THAT WAS MINE, TOO

Sometimes *pretending* you had a senior moment can save the day. Raconteur and Republican senator from New York Chauncey M. Depew was chosen to speak after Mark Twain at a banquet. As Depew watched, Twain delivered an uproarious talk. Depew walked to the dais, waited until the laughter and applause had died down, and then cannily feigned forgetfulness. "Mr. Toastmaster and Ladies and Gentlemen," he announced, "before this dinner Mark Twain and myself agreed to trade speeches. He has just delivered my speech, and I am gratified for the pleasant way in which you received it. I regret to say that I have lost the notes of *his* speech and cannot remember anything he was to say. Thank you."

"HOPE YOU LIKE IT!"

English clergyman and writer William Lisle Bowles once gave a parishioner a copy of the Bible as a birthday present. When she asked him to write an inscription, he signed it "From the Author."

DOES THAT MEAN I DON'T HAVE YOUR VOTE?

The late Tennessee senator Howard Baker was once walking from the Senate floor to his office when a group of tourists stopped him. One man said, "Say, I know who you are.  Don't tell me. Let me remember. I'll get it in a minute." Baker waited patiently for the man's memory to return. Finally, the senator said, "Howard Baker." The tourist shook his head, still in the grip of his senior moment: "No, that's not it."

SACRE BLEU! IS NOTHING . . . *SACRE*?

Changing the French language is such a sensitive subject (at least in France) that when the French broadcaster TF1 reported in 2016 that the spelling and/or accent marks of some 2,400 words might be altered in an attempt to modernize them, there was a fierce outcry. The Académie française's last complete dictionary came out in 1935, and work on the "new" edition had only reached the letter R, so it wasn't surprising that any change at all would make waves. One critic called it "the true beginning of anarchy." But even the most fervent believers in the power of tradition didn't reckon on the even greater power of absentmindedness. In a widely circulated petition, a national group of university students accused the education minister, who had authorized the spelling changes, of abusing her power. The outraged students must have forgotten to check their Académie française dictionary. They misspelled the verb "to authorize."

ON SECOND THOUGHT,
DON'T BRING HIM BACK

They say that sequels are never as good as the original, but rarely are they as bad as *Bring Back Birdie*, the follow-up to the classic musical *Bye Bye Birdie*. Legendary song-and-dance man Donald O'Connor was picked to play former teen idol Conrad Birdie 20 years after the events of the first play. Birdie was now supposed to be a middle-aged small-town mayor who had just been talked into making a comeback. But one night during the show's short (*very* short) run—four performances in all—O'Connor forgot all the words to one song. He stood silently on stage, miserable and disgusted with both himself and the play, and said to the musicians in the pit, "*You* sing it. I hate this song anyway," and then walked off.

OR WOULD YOU PREFER "ROBERT"?

Once, the hopelessly absentminded jazz great Benny Goodman telephoned George Simon, a famous editor of a jazz magazine. Goodman admitted to him sheepishly, "Whenever I call your house, I'm always embarrassed if your wife answers because I can't remember her last name." Then Goodman asked George for help. "What is her name, Bob?"

AND, WHILE YOU'RE AT IT, DO YOU MIND LOOKING AT MY TOASTER OVEN?

During a meeting of county commissioners, the controller in Reading, Pennsylvania, complained that her computer hadn't worked in two years, and that during the entire time she had been forced to use a typewriter for all her letters and memos. She probably would have had grounds for some legal action had it not been for the discovery soon after that she had forgotten to plug in her computer.

NEXT TIME I'LL WEAR
A COAT WITH A ZIPPER

Essayist Charles Lamb encountered Samuel Coleridge one day on Hampstead Heath in London. Coleridge took hold of one of the buttons on Lamb's coat, pulled him aside, and began to expound on a subject that was on his mind. A short time later, Lamb remembered that he was due elsewhere. Seeing no other means of escape, he took out his pocketknife and cut off the button that Coleridge was still clutching, leaving it in the poet's hand. Some hours later, Lamb returned to find Coleridge in the same spot, talking to himself on the same subject. Lamb then took up his former position while Coleridge, with the button still in his hand, continued to hold forth, apparently not having noticed his friend's absence.

YES, BUT LANDLORDS LOVE ME

Thomas De Quincey, the author of *Confessions of an English Opium-Eater*, was so absentminded that he often had trouble with the most straightforward tasks. He needed help dressing himself, and while looking over manuscripts by candlelight, he sometimes forgot what he was doing and set fire to his hair. A prodigious collector of books, he would stuff his apartment with them until every last nook and cranny was filled, at which point he would resort to an ingenious solution: He would abandon the entire collection and move to another apartment.

EVERYONE SING ALONG: "LET'S GET FISCAL, FISCAL! I WANNA GET FISCAL!"

It's frustrating when the wrong word or pronunciation slips out of your mouth before you can catch it. Now imagine if you had to experience these verbal slips day after day, coming from dozens of other people. When Tracy McCreery, a state representative from St. Louis, couldn't take it anymore, she filed a resolution in 2016 begging her colleagues in the Missouri legislature to stop saying "physical" when they meant to say "fiscal." It's like "nails on a chalkboard," she told the *Riverfront Times*. "There are a lot of reasons to be depressed about the Missouri legislature, and this just kind of piles on."

B = SECOND SHELF FROM TOP[2]

Photographer Ernst Haas took a famous picture of Albert Einstein, which shows the great physicist thoughtfully rubbing his chin, as if he were pondering the mysteries of the universe. But in fact, the picture was taken right after Haas asked Einstein where on the shelf he had put a particular book.

YOU MEAN WE'RE GOING TO A REAL JAIL?

A man attempting to rob a Bank of America branch in Merced, California, didn't have a gun, so he tried what he thought was the next best thing: He stuck his finger in his jacket pocket and pointed it at the teller. The man then experienced an incredible senior moment: He took his finger out of his pocket and pointed it at the teller, demanding money. He even cocked his thumb. The teller, trying not to laugh, told him to wait and called the police, who arrested him—using real handcuffs.

INCIDENTALLY, WHO'S THE PIANIST THIS EVENING?

One evening at a concert, the Polish-born pianist Josef Casimir Hofmann sat down at his piano with a look of confusion. The other members of the orchestra

waited, becoming increasingly alarmed. Finally, Hofmann leaned toward a woman in the first row of the audience and whispered, "May I please see your program, madam? I forget what comes first."

AT LEAST THEY DIDN'T BRING FILTHY LUCRE

What better way to make an advertisement stand out in a crowded marketplace than to use some colorful, imaginative slang? That, at least, was the hope of Silo, a discount electronics chain that ran a TV commercial in Seattle and El Paso offering a stereo system for the low, low price of "299 bananas." What the chain forgot was that some people have no imagination—or maybe too much. Dozens of people lined up outside the stores, not with dollars, but with bags of bananas. Silo was forced to honor the offer, and lost thousands of dollars before they were finally able to cancel the ad.

NEXT WEEK WE'LL BE HONORING
SERGEANT WOOLWORTHS

Britain's greatest World War II general, Field Marshal Bernard Law Montgomery, was attending a 1946 dinner given in his honor in Hollywood by MGM's Samuel Goldwyn.

Famous for his senior moments, Goldwyn began his introduction ably: "It gives me great pleasure tonight to welcome to Hollywood a very distinguished soldier." He then raised his glass and said to the gathering of celebrities, "Ladies and gentlemen, I propose a toast to . . . Marshall Field Montgomery." There was a stunned silence, since Marshall Field was and is a famous department store in Chicago. Into the breach came another mogul with a bad memory, Jack Warner of Warner Bros., who called out helpfully, "Montgomery Ward, you mean."

ROYALLY SCREWED UP

Sometimes a senior moment that should have led to an utter debacle is neatly handled by quick thinking and hard earned experience. Lawrence Barrett, a great 19th-century actor and theater manager, was forced to hire an elderly friend at the last minute to replace someone in the important role of the king. The friend's role was to shout out orders to Barrett, but when the time came for the old actor to begin, the senior citizen experienced a very senior moment. At a loss, he ad-libbed to Barrett, "Come here!" Expecting the worst, Barrett walked over to the throne. His friend whispered into his ear that he couldn't remember a single line. At a complete loss, Barrett bowed and headed off stage. But just as Barrett approached the wings, he heard a royal command from his old friend: "Forget nothing I have told you!" The audience never suspected that anything was wrong.

THE SECOND ANNUAL
G. K. CHESTERTON AWARD
FOR ABSENTMINDEDNESS
GOES TO . . . G. K. CHESTERTON!

One day British writer G. K. Chesterton was hurrying down the street, late for a critically important appointment. But first, finding himself thirsty, he stopped off for some refreshment, a glass of milk at the local dairy that he had visited as a child. Next, he bought a revolver at a gunsmith's shop, which he had been meaning to do for some time. Only then did he manage to remember where he was supposed to be going—his own wedding.

AT LEAST I THINK HE'S DEAD

Senator Bob Dole's speech-making ability wasn't helped by his lapses of memory. He once sought to explain the difficulty faced by politicians who were intent on keeping their private lives private. "You read what Disraeli had to say," he declared, and then paused at some length. "I don't remember what he said. He said something." Another pause, then, "He's no longer with us."

AT LEAST IT WAS PADDED

One evening, Hans Hotter, the bass-baritone whose most famous role was Wotan, the German god, in Wagner's opera *Die Walküre*, was getting ready to make his grand entrance in Act III. He absentmindedly grabbed his cloak from his dressing room, flung it around his shoulders, and strode onto the stage, whereupon the audience began to snicker. Sticking out of the back of the cloak was the padded pink coat hanger it had been hanging on.

WAIT TILL YOU SEE WHAT I'M GETTING FOR YOU NEXT WEEK

When he was the Democratic Senate majority leader, Lyndon Johnson ran into New Hampshire Republican Norris Cotton in the Senate elevator. "Norris," cried LBJ, "I've been looking for you. Come into my office." Johnson took a small box from his desk and presented it to Cotton with great fanfare. "Norris, when I was in Mexico recently, I had some cuff links made to give to a few personal friends in the Senate, and this is the first opportunity I have had to present them to you." Cotton told Johnson he was touched and would always cherish them. About three weeks later, Cotton bumped into LBJ again. Johnson grabbed him and cried, "Norris, I've been looking for you. Come into my office." For the second time, Johnson presented him with a small box. It was another pair of cuff links. "Norris," he said, "when I was in Mexico recently, I had some cuff links made to give to a few personal friends in the Senate . . ."

AND THE GUY STANDING NEXT TO YOU IS MARC ANTONY

Twentieth Century Fox Studios chief Spyros Skouras had a terrible memory for names. One day on the set of *Cleopatra*, a female cast member came up to him and said, "You don't know my name, do you?" "Yes, I do," he lied. The beautiful actress taunted him. "You're paying me $1 million and you can't remember my name! Spyros, tell me my name! I'll give you half the money back!" said Elizabeth Taylor. Skouras struggled to remember. "Ehh . . . ehh . . . you are Cleopatra!"

LET'S SEE, THAT WOULD MAKE IT FOUR-THIRTY IN JERUSALEM

In Cecil B. DeMille's film *The Crusades*, Henry Wilcoxon, who played King Richard the Lionhearted, forgot what century he was in. When he tossed back his cloak, the audience got a good look at his wristwatch.

WE HATE TO THINK WHAT SHE PUTS IN HER TEA

Elizabeth Morrow, poet, educator, and wife of Senator Dwight Morrow, invited the all-powerful banker J. P. Morgan to tea one day. Morgan possessed a huge, purple-hued nose that was almost as celebrated as his great wealth. Mrs. Morrow carefully coached her daughters not to comment on it, no matter how odd it might look to them. She was especially worried about what her daughter Anne might say. Anne, who later married Charles Lindbergh and became a bestselling writer, was known for speaking her mind. Anne couldn't take her eyes off Morgan's nose, but she and the other girls were quickly introduced to Morgan and ushered out of the room before they could do any damage. It was only then that Elizabeth Morrow relaxed her guard. "So, Mr. Morgan," she asked the esteemed guest, "will you have cream or lemon in your nose?"

OTHER THAN THAT,
I THINK I'M UP TO SPEED

When Prime Minister Benjamin Disraeli tried to visit his friend Lady Bradford, he was told by her servant that she had gone into town, as she usually did on Mondays. "I thought you would know that, sir," the servant said. "I did not," replied Disraeli, "nor did I know that it was Monday."

STRIKE THAT LAST REMARK
FROM THE RECORD

Australian judge Dean Mildren once declared from the bench that he was "absolutely staggered" that a notorious burglar had been freed on bail for the third time in a year, even after flagrantly ignoring a court-imposed curfew. Mildren demanded to know the identity of the idiot jurist. He was quietly reminded that he was the idiot.

RECYCLING

Although Arthur James, who taught classics at Eton for many years, could quote the great works of ancient Greece and Rome from memory, he was plagued by senior moments after his retirement. One day, when James was cycling home, he met a friend who noted that James had gotten a new bicycle. James looked down in confusion and realized that he must have taken the postmaster's bicycle by mistake. So he cycled to the post office, which was seven miles away, leaned the bicycle against the wall, went inside, apologized to the postmaster, went back outside, got back on the man's bicycle, and rode home.

AT LEAST THEY DIDN'T DROP ANY BATS

What better way to promote a baseball team than to shower fans with money? After one game, the West Michigan Whitecaps, a minor league team in the

Detroit Tigers system, had a helicopter drop $1,000 in various denominations onto the field. Unfortunately, the team forgot just how much people loved money. In the mad scramble to grab some cash, several kids were hurt badly enough to need medical treatment. But there was one thing the team's management did remember: Everyone who bought a ticket to the game had waived his or her right to sue.

THE UNEXPECTED IS *ALWAYS* LIKELY TO HAPPEN

Every veteran sportscaster has suffered an occasional senior moment, but precious few have had as many as British announcer John Matson, who has delighted his listeners with such pearls as: "In a sense, it's a one-man show, except there are two men involved, Hartson and Berkovic, and a third man, the goalkeeper!"; "Bruce has the taste of victory in his nostrils!"; and "The goals made such a difference to the way this game went!"

I WAS SO MUCH OLDER THEN,
I'M EVEN OLDER THAN THAT NOW

Years after writing and recording his classic hit "Maggie Mae," Rod Stewart revealed that the song had been inspired by his first true love—whose real name, alas, he could no longer remember.

IT'S A GOOD THING HE COULD
REMEMBER FLIGHT NUMBERS

When Dr. John Fellows bought a round-trip ticket from London to New York to pay a surprise visit to his daughter, he had no idea how surprised *he* would be. First, the absentminded doctor could not remember his daughter's address upon landing. Then he could not remember her phone number. "I was tired," he explained later. And so he did what anyone suffering from an especially exhausting trip, coupled with an especially bad senior moment, would have done in the same situation: He caught the next plane home.

THAT IS TO SAY, YOUR EX–GOOD FRIEND ELLIOT MENDELSON

When the famously distracted Hungarian mathematician Paul Erdös met a colleague at a conference, Erdös asked the other man where he was from. "Vancouver," he replied. "Oh, then you must know my good friend Elliot Mendelson," Erdös remarked. His colleague gave him a funny look. "I *am* your good friend Elliot Mendelson!"

LOVELY THRONE, YOUR MAJESTY, BUT WHAT EXACTLY DOES THIS SWITCH DO?

When the Abyssinian emperor Menelik II decided to modernize his country in 1890, he personally ordered three electric chairs from New York, for truly modern executions. But it had slipped the emperor's mind that his country had no electricity. As a result, two of the chairs were quickly disposed of. The third, however, served nicely as the emperor's throne.

OH, THAT EXPLAINS WHY
HE ASKED ME FOR A DOUBLE

In the 1920s, movie star Douglas Fairbanks was driving back to his Beverly Hills estate when he passed a man with a familiar face and an aristocratic bearing who was walking down the road on a hot day. Fairbanks stopped to offer him a ride, which the surprised man accepted gratefully in an educated British accent. Unable to remember the man's name, but convinced he knew him from somewhere, Fairbanks invited him inside his mansion for a drink. During their conversation, the visitor seemed to know a lot of Fairbanks's friends and was even familiar with the mansion itself, as if he had visited it often. Fairbanks eventually managed to whisper to his secretary, "Who is this Englishman? I know he's Lord Somebody, but I can't remember his name." "That," replied the secretary, "is the English butler you fired last month for getting drunk."

NEXT WEEK: FOOLPROOF TIPS
FOR REMEMBERING APPOINTMENTS

The members of the Oxford Library Club for Retired Professional People and Others Interested were especially looking forward to hearing a guest speaker on the subject of "Old Age, Absent-Mindedness, and Keeping Fit." Unfortunately, the speaker forgot to turn up.

ALTHOUGH THEY DID CRUSH THEIR
LAST PRECIOUS BAG OF CHIPS

Two New Zealand botanists spent years searching their country's wetlands for an extremely rare flower, the aptly named "swamp helmet orchid," which they feared might already be extinct. Then one day the tired, hungry, and dispirited botanists sat down to take a lunch break, and when they got up, discovered that they had been sitting on the flower all that time. (Fortunately, the orchid was unharmed, or else the furor would never have . . . uh . . . died out.)

AT FIRST THE FLIGHT
JUST SEEMED BORING . . .

It was a routine Northwest Airlines flight in 2009 from San Diego to Minneapolis. At least it *was* routine until the plane flew past the Minneapolis airport and kept going for another 150 miles. An emergency at the airport? An emergency on the airplane? No, just a really bad case of absentmindedness. The captain and first officer were so busy looking at a new crew schedule on their laptop that they forgot to look up and check where they were or respond to air traffic control. It was only when a flight attendant called on the intercom to ask what was happening that they snapped out of it, turned around, and flew back to Minneapolis—just before fighter jets were about to be sent aloft to intercept the plane, for fear it had been hijacked.

AT LEAST I REMEMBERED
THAT I FORGOT THEM

"Many years ago," Harpo Marx recalled late in life, "a very wise man named Bernard Baruch (the great financier and presidential adviser) took me aside and put his arm around my shoulder. 'Arthur, my boy,' he said, 'I'm going to give you three pieces of advice, three things you should always remember.' My heart jumped and I glowed with expectation. I was going to hear the magic passwords to a rich, full life from the master himself. 'Yes, sir?' I said. And he told me the three things. I regret that I've forgotten what they were."

A BRIDGE TOO FAR

When the Intermarine Company of Ameglia, Italy, landed a multimillion dollar contract to build a minesweeper and three military launches in their shipyard for the Malaysian government, everything seemed fine. But then the people in charge of the project remembered that the river connecting the shipyard to the sea was spanned by a very low bridge under which the ships would not be able to pass. The company offered to knock the bridge down and rebuild it after the ships were safely on their way, but the town refused, having grown more attached to the bridge than to the company.

AT LEAST HE DIDN'T DO THAT THING WHERE HE SHAKES THE WATER OFF

Philosopher Irwin Edman often used the pool of his friend and neighbor, publisher Robert Haas. One day, after finishing his laps, Edman wandered into Haas's living room and picked up a copy of *The History of the Peloponnesian War* by Thucydides. Forgetting that he was still in his wet bathing suit, the professor leafed through a few pages and then began to read. Later, after he'd left, Mrs. Haas arrived home. Furious, she called for the maid and pointed at the living room floor. "It's that dog again," she seethed. "No, Madame," the maid explained, "not the dog. It's the professor."

WHEN I'M PRESIDENT, I SWEAR THIS SORT OF THING WON'T HAPPEN

Abraham Lincoln served as a captain during the Black Hawk War of 1832. One day he found himself leading a militia company across a field and toward a gate. The proper command for directing the troops through the gate escaped him completely. "This company is dismissed for two minutes," he finally shouted in desperation, "and will fall in again on the other side of the gate!"

FLATTERY WILL GET YOU
EVERYWHERE—OR AT LEAST
OFF THE HOOK

When he was having a senior moment and couldn't place people, journalist Charles Michelson, FDR's speechwriter and the publicity director of the Democratic Party for thirty years, used this ploy to avoid offending them. When a person asked, "Do you remember me?" he would always answer, "Yes, and it turned out you were right, didn't it?"

HOW MANY DAKOTAS
ARE THERE, AGAIN?

It's hard to remember certain facts and figures without referring to notes, but you'd think a presidential candidate crisscrossing the country could remember the number of states in the United States. On the campaign trail in 2008, Barack Obama said, " . . . it is just wonderful to be back in Oregon, and over the last fifteen months we've traveled to every corner of the United States. I've now been in fifty-seven states—I think one left to go."

ALTHOUGH AN OFFICE IN OMAN MIGHT NOT BE A BAD IDEA

Editors are expected to have excellent memories and fact-checking skills—unless they're editing the magazine *Business Insurance*, which was forced to publish this *mea culpa*: "The following corrects the errors in the July 17 Geographical Agent and Broker listing: Aberdeen is in Scotland, not Saudi Arabia or England; Antwerp is in Belgium, not Barbados; Baie Mahault is in Guam, not Guadeloupe; Belfast is in Northern Ireland, not Nigeria; Bogotá was listed twice in Colombia; Cardiff is in Wales, not Vietnam; Edinburgh is in Scotland, not England; Helsinki is in Finland, not Fiji; Moscow is in Russia, not Qatar; [and] Nilsen Brothers has an office in Norway, not Oman."

WHERE THE TWO OF US WILL TALK ABOUT HOW CRAZY YOU ARE

Clergyman, writer, and famed wit Sydney Smith described the English politician Lord Dudley Stuart as one of the most absentminded men he had ever met. "One day he met me in the street and invited me to meet myself: 'Dine with me today; dine with me, and I will get Sydney Smith to meet you.' I admitted the temptation he held out to me, but said I was engaged to meet him elsewhere."

WOULD IT HAVE HURT TO ASK FOR DIRECTIONS?

In one of the greatest senior moments in sports history, Jim Marshall of the Minnesota Vikings snatched up a fumbled football in a game against the San Francisco 49ers on October 25, 1964, and started running the wrong way. That was bad enough, but on his 60-yard journey, Marshall didn't seem to grasp that his opponents showed no interest in stopping him. Worse, he ignored his own teammates, who raced after him shouting and motioning for him to turn around. When Marshall finally crossed his own team's goal line, scoring a safety—two points—for the other team, 49er Bruce Bosley hugged him.

FOR MY NEXT TRICK, I'LL BURY MYSELF IN THE WRONG GRAVE

The Irish writer Charles Maturin, famous for his horror stories, was also well known for his mental lapses. He was often seen wearing a boot on one foot and a shoe on the other, and sometimes turned up at parties one or two days late. He once sent a novel to his publishers in several packages, but neglected to include page numbers. And so it came as no surprise to his friends that his death was hastened when he took the wrong medicine by mistake.

THE VERY LONG GOOD-BYE

An absentminded young woman was about to take her leave of the essayist Agnes Repplier in the writer's Philadelphia apartment. At least it seemed that way to Repplier, who was sharper and wittier than most of her younger admirers before she died in her nineties. Reluctant to leave, the visitor picked up her hat and scarf and then put them down again. She shifted her feet back and forth. She gazed around the room distractedly. Finally she said, "There was something I meant to say, but I've forgotten what it was." "Perhaps, my dear," Repplier suggested helpfully, "it was good-bye."

AND IS COLONEL PANTS WELL?

Theodore Roosevelt prided himself on his memory for names and faces, although he was just as vulnerable to senior moments as anyone else. At a White House dinner one evening, he stood shaking hands with a long line of visitors. When it was the turn of a man from New York who specialized in custom-made shirts, the haberdasher asked, "Do you remember me, Mr. President? I make your shirts." "Major Schurtz?" boomed Roosevelt, who had known the man for years. "Why, of course I remember, Major! And how are all the boys of the old regiment?"

THOSE WHO MISLAY THE PAST ARE DOOMED TO FORGET IT

Like many communities, residents of Wilkinsburg, Pennsylvania, decided to prepare and bury a time capsule for the people of the future. It was buried in 1962 and was supposed to be dug up twenty-five years later during the town's centennial, but when 1987 rolled around, all the people involved in filling the capsule had died. Since they also had forgotten to write down its location, the ceremony to dig up the container had to be canceled.

LET'S SEE NOW, WHICH ONES GO "*BAA*" AND WHICH GO "*MOO*"?

At the Institute for Animal Health in Edinburgh, Scotland, scientists were studying whether the country's sheep could have been infected with mad cow disease. They had already spent four years in extensive testing when investigators discovered that someone had absentmindedly mixed up cow brains with sheep brains in the freezer, after someone else had mislabeled them.

AND THE CHILDREN SHALL LEAD US

When the family of MIT mathematician Norbert Wiener moved from Cambridge, Massachusetts, to the nearby suburb of Newton, his wife knew the famously absentminded professor would never be able to find his way to the new place on his own. So she wrote down the Newton address on a piece of paper and gave it to him before he left that first morning. A few hours later, when an idea struck him, he found the piece of paper in his pocket and scribbled some notes on the back. After he looked over the notes, however, he decided his idea was worthless, and threw the paper away. With no note to remind him he had moved, he returned to his old house in Cambridge to be met by his daughter, waiting there for him. "Hi, Daddy," she said. "Mommy thought you would forget."

STOP ME IF YOU'VE HEARD THE ONE ABOUT ALL THE KING'S HORSES

Britain's Charles II, who reigned from 1660 to 1685, loved telling anecdotes about his past. His courtiers, who had heard the stories many times, found them so boring that they tried to escape if they could. The Earl of Rochester, for one, wondered how a man who could remember every last detail of a story couldn't recall that he had told it to the very same people the day before.

WHO DO YOU THINK WE ARE? GEOGRAPHERS?

The disaster movie *Krakatoa: East of Java* is about the devastating eruption of a volcanic island and the tsunami that followed. Alas, no one in Hollywood remembered to check a map before the film went into production. Krakatoa is actually *west* of Java.

I ALSO DINED LAST WEEK

The classics scholar Richard Porson, who held the prestigious Regius Professorship in Greek at Cambridge University, never remembered to answer letters. Sometimes he remained incommunicado for days or even weeks on end, having forgotten to tell colleagues what he would be doing, where he would be staying, or when he would reappear. Once, when asked to dinner by a friend, he replied absentmindedly, "Thank you, no. I dined yesterday."

NO STARCH, AND MAKE SURE
YOU TAKE EVERYTHING
OUT OF THE POCKETS

Since the Cuban Missile Crisis in October of 1962, every U.S. president has been accompanied at all times by an armed military officer carrying an impenetrable titanium briefcase known as the "nuclear football." The briefcase contains the codes needed to launch a missile strike. The president also carries an "authenticator ID" that must be used in conjunction with the codes—unless, of course, he forgets where he put it. President Jimmy Carter did. He left it in the pocket of one of his suits, which was then sent off to be dry cleaned.

TWO OUT OF THREE, *MON AMI*?

In 17th-century France, the Comte de Brancas was playing backgammon when he asked for a glass of wine. He proceeded to gulp down the dice and throw the wine on the board, soaking his opponent in the process.

TERRIBLY, TERRIBLY SORRY
ABOUT YOUR DEATH

Having attended the University of
Edinburgh, Henry Erskine, Lord
Advocate of Scotland in the late 18th
century, would occasionally return to the
university to visit his old friends. One day
he met an especially absentminded, now
elderly, tutor of whom he was very fond.
He was taken aback when the man greeted
him by saying, "I was very sorry, my dear
boy, that you have had the fever in your
family. Was it you or your brother who
died of it?" Bemused, Erskine replied
that it was he who had died. "Ah, dear
me, I thought so," the tutor said sadly.
"Very sorry for it," he kept muttering as
he went on his way. "Very sorry for it."

NO HAIR APPARENT

John Drew, a comic stage actor, once
shaved off his mustache, dramatically
changing his appearance. Soon after, he

met Max Beerbohm, the English satirist, whom he failed to remember. Beerbohm, on the other hand, remembered the American. "Mr. Drew," he said, "I'm afraid you don't recognize me without your mustache."

OR MAYBE YOU SHOULD GIVE POLITICS A TRY

In 1943, Warner Bros. released the musical comedy *This Is the Army*, written by Irving Berlin and costarring First Lieutenant Ronald Reagan. During the first week of shooting, Reagan was introduced to Berlin five different times, and Berlin said the same thing each time: "Young man, I just saw some of your work. You've got a few things to correct—for example, a huskiness of the voice—but you really should give this business some consideration when the war is over." Reagan had already been working in Hollywood for six years.

MAKING DEMOCRACY
ALMOST WORK

Herbert Connolly remembered to do almost everything a politician could do to win a seat on the Massachusetts Governors Council in 1988. He campaigned hard, even on the day of the election. He made speeches everywhere. He shook thousands of hands. He personally urged everyone he met to rush to the polls. He forgot just one small thing: to get to his own neighborhood polling station before it closed so he could vote for himself. Nevertheless, with all his hard work, he got 14,715 votes. Unfortunately, his opponent got 14,716.

AT LEAST WE GOT
THE NUMBERS RIGHT

Some misspellings are so impressive that they're way up there on the "senior moments scale." Consider the case of the highway sign erected in 2009 on Interstate

39 near the towns of Rothschild and Schofield in Wisconsin. The only word that was spelled correctly was the first. It read, EXIT 185 BUISNESS 51 ROTHSCHIELD SCHOFEILD.

IT WAS, PERHAPS, THE BEST FAMILY I'VE EVER TASTED

King Edward VII, Britain's king from 1901 to 1910, once tried to remember a visit he made to the home of Colonel James Biddle, during which he was served a dish of seasoned pork and cornmeal hardened into a loaf, then sliced and fried, known as scrapple. "In Philadelphia, when I was the Prince of Wales, I met a large and interesting family named Scrapple," he recalled hazily. "They served me a rather delicious native food, too—something, I believe, called Biddle."

GUYS—THEY'RE ALL ALIKE

In 2006, Guy Goma, who had moved from Congo to England, was thrilled to get an interview with the BBC for a job as an entry-level information technology (IT) assistant. As Goma sat in a waiting room, another Guy, Guy Kewney, a well-known IT consultant, was also at the station, waiting to be interviewed on live television. But when an absentminded assistant arrived, he led the wrong Guy to the studio. After greeting Goma, the TV interviewer wasted no time, asking him if he thought more people would now be downloading content online. Goma gamely tried to answer: "I think it is much better for the development and . . . uh . . . to inform people what they want and to get the easy way and so faster if they are looking for." (Goma was finally interviewed for the IT job afterward, but sadly, even after his 15 minutes of TV fame, he wasn't hired.)

WHILE WE'RE AT IT, LET'S CHANGE GRANTHAM TO . . . GRANTHAM!

In the late 1980s the town of Grantham, New Hampshire, finally decided to clear up the confusion that two streets with similar names, Stoney Brook Drive and Stoney Brook Lane, caused its residents. But the Grantham town council then forgot the point of renaming the streets in the first place, dubbing them Old Springs Drive and Old Springs Lane.

AH! THAT WOULD EXPLAIN THE STRANGE HAT I'M WEARING

Pope John XXIII, who was pontiff from 1958 until his death in 1963, once said that while he was falling asleep, important thoughts would drift through his mind and he would try to make a mental note: "I must speak to the pope about that." Then, he explained, "I would be wide awake and remember, 'I *am* the pope!'"

NOW, *THAT'S* ACTING

One day the famous British actor John Gielgud was dining in a restaurant with a well-known playwright when Gielgud spied someone he thought he recognized. "Did you see that man just coming in?" he asked his companion. "He's the biggest bore in London, second only to Edward Knoblock." It was precisely at that moment that he realized that the man sitting across from him was none other than Edward Knoblock. "Not you, of course," Gielgud quickly added. "I mean the *other* Edward Knoblock."

NO DOMESTIC PAWN

In 1937, chess master George Koltanowski simultaneously defeated thirty-four players while blindfolded, a world record. But when he died, his wife Leah said that Koltanowski never once remembered to bring home bread from the grocery.

AND THAT'S SPELLED L-A-M-P-E

After German philosopher Immanuel Kant fired his longtime servant, Lampe, he feared that the man would remain in his memory forever. A little guilt, perhaps? So Kant wrote in his journal, "Remember in the future the name of Lampe must be completely forgotten."

HOW CAN I BE SURE?

Jesse Lasky, whose career as a Hollywood producer and studio executive stretched from 1913 to 1951, was making a speech welcoming French actor and singer Maurice Chevalier at a dinner in New York when he kept losing his place. Each time, he looked up in confusion and said, "Now where was I?" He did this so many times that comedian George Jessel finally called out, "You're at the Hotel Astor and your name is Jesse Lasky."

I'D LIKE TO MEET THAT MAN
SOME DAY

Franz Schubert's friends were amazed that he often seemed to be in a trance when he wrote music and afterward did not remember what he had done. One day the baritone Vogl sang one of Schubert's songs, and when he was finished, Schubert exclaimed, "That's not bad! Who wrote it?"

SPACE, THE FINAL FRONTIER OF
MEMORY LAPSES—MISSION 1

University of Idaho scientist David Atkinson devoted much of his working life to designing an experiment for an unmanned European space mission to Saturn. The mission was to measure the winds on Titan, Saturn's largest moon. In 1997, the probe was launched. Eight years later, on January 14, 2005, Atkinson and his team waited anxiously for the first data to arrive. And then waited, and waited some more to no avail. Too bad someone forgot to turn on the measuring equipment before the takeoff all those years before.

IN THAT CASE I'M GOING TO MOVE TO *ANOTHER* TINY PACIFIC ISLAND NATION!

Edward Natapei, the prime minister of the tiny Pacific island nation of Vanuatu, lost his seat in Parliament, and thus his position as prime minister, all because of absentmindedness. Natapei missed three straight parliamentary sessions in 2009 while he was at an overseas conference. The problem? Under Vanuatu law, he was supposed to submit a written explanation for his absence to the country's parliamentary speaker, which he forgot to do.

THE WORD IS "CONFUSED"

Allen Ludden, the host of the TV game show *Password*, had a senior moment on the air that must have confused even the most adept puzzle solver: "Just remember, folks," he announced, "next Monday night's *Password* will be seen on Thursday evening."

AND WHENEVER I SAY ST. PAUL, I'LL MEAN MINNEAPOLIS

Dr. William Archibald Spooner, the absentminded Anglican priest and Oxford University administrator who gave his name to the linguistic lapses called "spoonerisms," once concluded a sermon by stating, "In the sermon I have just preached, whenever I said Aristotle, I meant St. Paul."

THEY BOTH BEGIN WITH
THE LETTER *M*, RIGHT?

If you do the same thing over and over until it becomes a reflex, beware of the consequences—it can lead to an embarrassing bout of absentmindedness. Consider the case of race car driver Lewis Hamilton. When he was just 10 years old, he told the founder of McLaren Automotive, the manufacturer of high performance vehicles, that he wanted to race for the company when he grew up. Four years later he joined McLaren's program for young drivers. In 2007, he made his Formula One debut, driving a McLaren. In 2008, he became world champion—for McLaren. And so in 2013, during a Grand Prix race in Malaysia, Hamilton pulled into the McLaren pit for a routine change of tires. There was just one problem: He was now driving for Mercedes.

WAIT, WHAT HAPPENED TO THE ACCORDION SOLO?

Fans of Lawrence Welk's easy-listening music were the victims of an especially cruel senior moment when some 10,000 copies of Welk's CD *Polka Party* were mislabeled. They were actually copies of the sound track to the film *Sid and Nancy* about the life and death of notorious punk rocker Sid Vicious.

AND THEN I PUT MY HEAD THROUGH THE WINDSHIELD, JUST FOR THE HELL OF IT

The year 1977 was a big one for senior moments involving Canadian drivers. According to the *Toronto Sun*, one driver, filling out an insurance claim form, explained his mishap this way: "Coming home I drove into the wrong house and collided with a tree I don't have." About the same time, another unfortunate driver wrote on his claim form, "I thought my window was down but I found out that it was up when I put my head through it."

CLEARLY HE WAS SAFER IN PRISON

In 2009, the newly appointed head of London's Metropolitan Police, Sir Paul Stephenson, personally led an early morning raid to catch the leader of a notorious burglary ring. Eighty officers swooped down on a suspected hideout as a police helicopter hovered overhead. Next, a battering ram made quick work of the front door. It was only when the police got inside that Sir Paul learned that the ringleader wasn't actually there. It seems no one remembered to do a final search of the police database to make sure of his whereabouts. If they had, they would have learned that he was already in prison, having been arrested five hours earlier in another raid carried out by constables from the local precinct.

ON THE WHOLE, I'D RATHER BE IN THE BLACK

Terrified of finding himself in a strange city without money, W. C. Fields opened a bank account in every town he visited. Moreover, he used a different name for each account because he was

fearful of being robbed. Unfortunately, because he never bothered to write down the aliases, he eventually forgot all but 23 of them—out of an estimated 700.

GENERAL MEMORY LOSS

Sir William Erskine was a senior commander under the Duke of Wellington. During one of Erskine's more appalling senior moments, he was found eating dinner instead of defending a strategic bridge. He later had second thoughts about neglecting the bridge, but dispatched only five men. When an officer expressed his concern that the bridge wasn't sufficiently defended, Erskine changed his mind again and decided he would send an entire regiment. He wrote a note to himself as a reminder, put it in his pocket, and then forgot all about it.

IT COULD HAVE BEEN WORSE— HE COULD HAVE LEFT OUT THE SECOND "H"

Dan O'Connor, a rabid Notre Dame football fan, decided to have the team's slogan, "Fighting Irish," tattooed on his arm. But the tattoo artist picked the wrong time to have a senior moment. Even with the design right in front of him, he inscribed the words, "Fighing Irish." O'Connor, who filed a suit for damages, reportedly said, "You're not talking about a dented car where you can get another one. You're talking about flesh."

THE THIRD ANNUAL
G. K. CHESTERTON AWARD
FOR ABSENTMINDEDNESS
GOES TO . . . G. K. CHESTERTON!

English writer G. K. Chesterton was especially baffled by trains. He once went up to a ticket window at a railroad station and asked the mystified agent for a cup of coffee, then retired to the station restaurant to wait for his train and tried to buy a ticket from the waiter.

WE WERE SO DESPERATE,
WE DIDN'T EVEN BOTHER
TO READ THEM FIRST

Entrepreneur Richard Branson, the founder of Virgin Records, Virgin America Airlines, Virgin Atlantic, and Virgin Mobile, is famous for his love of adventure. Having forgotten to take one essential item on an around-the-world balloon expedition, he offered this advice to fellow thrill-seekers: "If you're embarking around the world in a hot-air balloon, don't forget the toilet paper. Once, we had to wait for incoming faxes."

I'LL HAVE A POUND OF MAINSPRINGS, PLEASE

James Herriot was known for his absentmindedness in his small English village. When the famed veterinarian-turned-writer of *All Creatures Great and Small* arrived at the local butcher's shop with a broken clock under his arm, and then stood in front of the counter lost in thought, the butcher wasn't at all surprised. He just waited patiently for Herriot to order his usual pound of sausages. When Herriot finally snapped out of his reverie, he looked down and noticed the clock. Realizing that he was in the wrong shop, he nodded politely at the butcher and then, without a word, turned around and left.

DO NOT TAKE YOUR EYES OFF MY PLUME, SOLDIER, AND THAT'S AN ORDER

Alexander Borodin was a general in the Russian army, as well as a famous composer, chemist, and doctor. He once walked out of his home in full military dress. His jacket was adorned with medals, he wore a plumed helmet, and everything else necessary for a full-dress parade—except, that is, for his pants.

AND THAT'S WHEN I FIGURED OUT THAT WRITING THE WORDS WAS GOING TO BE EASIER THAN REMEMBERING THEM

The English novelist Paul Baily was once an actor, playing in *Richard III* at Stratford-upon-Avon, with Christopher Plummer in the leading role. In Act III, Scene V, Baily, playing the role of Lovell, was supposed to say, "Here is the head of that ignoble traitor, the dangerous and unsuspected Hastings." But one night, he couldn't remember the line at all. Plummer stared at him "for what seemed like ten minutes," Baily later said, and then Plummer declared, "Is that the head of that ignoble traitor, the dangerous and unsuspected Hastings?" to which the grateful Baily replied, to everyone's relief, "Yes."

GIVE OR TAKE A FEW ZEROS

Something must have slipped the collective mind of the former New York investment firm Bear Stearns when it ordered the sale of $4 billion worth of stock instead of the correct amount, $4 million, a 1,000-fold mistake. After its hideously expensive senior moment, the company was able to recover only about 85 percent of the mistakenly sold stock. And to think that a Bear Stearns advertisement had just boasted of the firm's ability to "execute complex transactions flawlessly."

AT LEAST HE'LL HAVE TIME
TO VISIT CARDIFF'S OFFICIAL
DOCTOR WHO SHOP

In 2007, Dave Barclay was determined to attend the July 6 wedding of his close friend, Dave Best. So he paid $1,000 for his plane ticket from Toronto to Wales (a hefty sum for a teacher) and cheerfully arrived in the Cardiff airport on July 6. He promptly asked for directions, and got to the venue eager for the great event, only to learn that he had forgotten to read his friend's invitation carefully. As it turned out, the wedding was scheduled for July 6 all right, but in *2008*.

WHAT ARE YOU SAYING—
THAT NEWSPAPERS
DON'T DELIVER THEMSELVES?

In 1965, publisher Lionel Burleigh launched the *Commonwealth Sentinel*, which, he claimed, would be "Britain's most fearless newspaper." Burleigh was staying at London's Brown's Hotel, frantically preparing for the paper's debut, when he received a call from the police: "Do you have anything to do with the *Commonwealth Sentinel*? Because there are 50,000 [copies] outside the hotel entrance and they're blocking the street." It seems that Burleigh had completely forgotten to arrange for the paper's distribution. As a result, the *Sentinel*, which was born on February 6, 1965, died on February 7.

OUR ACCOUNTANTS
ADVISED US NOT TO

Companies in Washington, D.C., mailed, as usual, their quarterly tax payments that were due on September 30 to a special post office box, only to have their envelopes returned, stamped: "Box Closed for Nonpayment of Rent." It seems that government officials had forgotten to pay the annual fee needed to keep the box open.

OH, YOU MEAN IN CASE OF AN *EXPECTED* EMERGENCY

It's always important to be prepared for disaster, as the folks in Alma, Alabama, know all too well. In May 2008, when a ferocious storm hit the town, twenty residents rushed to the community shelter which had just been built. Much to their dismay, however, the town leaders had forgotten to unlock it. The good folks of Alma were forced to sprawl on the ground behind the building as storm winds howled around them.

I KNEW THERE WAS SOMETHING VAGUELY FAMILIAR ABOUT ALL THAT BRILLIANT PROSE

When the absentminded Scottish writer John Campbell was in a bookstore one day, he became so engrossed in a book that it wasn't until he bought it, took it home, and read it halfway through that he realized he had written it himself.

BUT *IF* I HAD COMMITTED A CRIME, I WOULD HAVE PUNISHED MYSELF

When former New York mayor David Dinkins was accused of failing to pay his taxes, he blamed his poor memory. He had merely forgotten to do it, he explained, which made his sin one of omission, not commission—and thus not worth bothering about. "I haven't committed a crime," he stated forcefully. "What I did was fail to comply with the law."

THANKS, BUT I ALREADY HAVE A BOOKMARK JUST LIKE IT

When Albert Einstein received a $1,500 check from the Rockefeller Foundation as an honorarium, he used it as a bookmark for months, then lost the book. Trying to keep its records in order, the Foundation sent a duplicate check, and Einstein, having forgotten the first one, wrote back, "What's this for?"

JUST DON'T LET HIM TOUCH THE GROUND

At one memorable meeting, the members of the Republican caucus of Grand Rapids, Michigan, forgot to bring the American flag for the obligatory—and we mean *truly* obligatory—Pledge of Allegiance. The members were stymied until party member Jack Pettit, who happened to be wearing a stars-and-stripes necktie, climbed onto a chair and remained motionless while everyone recited the words.

NEXT STOP: AMNESIAVILLE

Traveling by train to attend a ceremony, the bishop of Exeter, William Cecil, couldn't find his ticket. "It's all right, my lord," said the sympathetic collector. "We know who you are." "That's all very well," replied the bishop, "but without my ticket, how am I to know where I'm going?"

THE PONY EXPRESS
IS LOOKING BETTER AND BETTER
ALL THE TIME

The United States's first airmail flight was scheduled to take off from Potomac Park in Washington, D.C., at 11:30 a.m. on May 15, 1918. You could feel the excitement: A large, expectant crowd had gathered, and even President Wilson was on hand. But the engine of the Curtiss Jenny airplane just wouldn't start. A squad of mechanics checked everything they could think of, but thirty minutes passed without success. The president was far from pleased—and he was even less pleased when a mechanic finally thought to check the fuel tank, which was empty.

THANK GOD WE FOUND A GAS STATION THAT WAS OPEN

When two robbers knocked off a gas station in Vancouver, Canada, they locked the attendant in the bathroom and drove off with $100. After driving around for a while, they realized they were lost and pulled back into the same station to ask for directions, failing to recognize either it or the attendant, who had just escaped from the bathroom. As they left the station for the second time, the attendant called the police. Amazingly, the clueless thieves then returned for a *third time*—now on foot. Their car had broken down a short distance away, they said, and they needed a tow.

HOW SOON THEY FORGET

When The History Channel in Great Britain conducted a poll asking viewers to rank the most important events in 20th-century British history, they must have forgotten quite a few. Topping the list,

and ranking above the First World War, the
Great Depression, the Second World War,
and the end of the Cold War, was the death
of Princess Diana back in 1997.

ANOTHER ROUND OF GROG, MATEY,
AND WE MIGHT GET
A STANDING OVATION

Actor Alan Devlin was known for
his habit of leaving the stage in a
fit of pique in mid-performance. Once,
while appearing in *H.M.S. Pinafore* at the
Dublin Gaiety Theatre, he looked out
at the audience and shouted, "I'm going
home! Finish it yourself!" But first he took
a detour. He went to Neary's bar in his
admiral's costume and ordered a round of
drinks. But Devlin had forgotten to take off
his radio mike, which was still turned on,
so the sounds of alcohol-fueled conversation
and clinking glasses filled the theater as
the dumbfounded cast and audience
listened in.

NAME ANOTHER PARTY

Before winning a senate seat in North
Carolina, future vice presidential
candidate John Edwards showed little
interest in politics and often forgot to
vote. He was once asked whether he had
started his political life by registering as
a Democrat or Republican. He couldn't
remember.

I'VE JUST HAD THE MOST
WONDERFUL CONVERSATION
WITH 894-606-5789

The brilliant Hungarian mathematician
Paul Erdös had the habit of phoning
colleagues around the world at all times
of the day. Although he could remember
the phone number of every mathematician
he knew, he frequently couldn't recall
their first names, so he didn't use them
in conversation—except for that of
one colleague, Tom Trotter, whom he
called Bill.

ON THE OTHER HAND, I CAN HEAR
A GUN COCKING 26 MILES AWAY

President Ulysses S. Grant had no ear for music, and no memory for it, either. When he was asked one evening if he had enjoyed a concert, he replied, "How could I? I know only two tunes. One of them is 'Yankee Doodle' and the other one isn't."

THOU SHALT REMEMBER!

Bill Harbach, one of the first executive producers of *The Tonight Show*, once attempted to ask his secretary to telephone future guest Charlton Heston to arrange a rehearsal. "Get me . . . uh . . . Charleston Huston!" Harbach barked. "Wait—I, uh, mean Charlton Hudson!" Suddenly recalling that the actor had starred as Moses in the movie *The Ten Commandments*, he corrected himself. "You know who I mean!" he told his secretary. "Chester Moses."

YOU THINK THIS IS BAD?
YOU SHOULD SEE WHAT I'M LIKE
WITH PARISHIONERS!

The 18th-century English vicar George Harvest was frequently forced to borrow a horse when he traveled because he had forgotten where he left his own. Eventually, people stopped lending him theirs because he mislaid those, too. When he did have his animal with him, he would dismount when he arrived at his destination and lead it away. But if the horse shook off the bridle or a stable boy removed it, the oblivious parson would continue to walk, holding the reins as if the horse were still attached.

WHAT ABOUT THE PAINTING OF THAT
WOMAN WITH THE ENIGMATIC SMILE?
DON'T TELL ME I OWN THAT ONE, TOO!

Eccentric publishing magnate William Randolph Hearst (1863–1951) was famous for his fanatical pursuit of art, which Orson Welles satirized in his film *Citizen Kane*. Once, Hearst sent an assistant to scour Europe for a masterpiece he was determined to add to his collection. Several months later, after he had looked everywhere, the man reported back that he'd finally located the item, and it would cost Hearst nothing! Why? Because the publisher had already bought it years before, stored it in a warehouse overseas, and then, as he had done with so many other things, forgotten all about it.

NOW, DON'T YOU FEEL BETTER?

Tatiana Cooley, the winner of several national memory contests, could remember a list of 3,125 words, 100 names and faces, 1,000 numbers, a 54-line poem, and the precise order of a shuffled deck of cards. But when it came to everyday life, she was notoriously absentminded and a chronic user of Post-it notes and lists.

AH, AND THAT WOULD EXPLAIN
WHY YOU'RE WEARING
THE MORE EXPENSIVE SUIT

Maxwell Perkins (1884–1947), the influential editor of F. Scott Fitzgerald, Ernest Hemingway, and Thomas Wolfe, was talking to a young writer one day when a distinguished-looking man entered Perkins's office at Charles Scribner's Sons, the New York publishing house. Perkins looked up at the man with no sign of recognition. Finally, the visitor could stand it no longer. "I'm Charles Scribner," Perkins's employer snapped.

AND MY NAME IS . . .
SEÑOR MOMENTO!

For a performance of Puccini's opera *Turandot*, the Rome Opera designed a set with a little stream and a small Chinese bridge that crossed over it. On one side of the stream was Carlos Gasparini, the tenor playing Prince Calaf, and on the other side, the soprano who played Princess Turandot. When she cried *"Mio nome è Amore!"* ("My name is love!"), he was supposed to run across the bridge and embrace her, but he forgot and tried to leap across the stream instead, tripped, and fell in.

YOU REALLY GOT ME SO I DON'T KNOW WHAT I'M DOING

When rock star Ray Davies of the Kinks took his driving test in the 1960s, he forgot to look where he was going and knocked down a woman carrying groceries. He jumped out of the car to help her, but forgot to put on the parking brake, forcing the driving 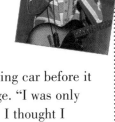 instructor to stop the moving car before it could do any more damage. "I was only learning to drive because I thought I should be a regular person," Davies said. "But that was stupid."

NO GENDER BIAS HERE

Ronald Reagan was famous for verbal senior moments years before his memory failed him completely. When he was hosting a White House state dinner for Prince Charles and Princess Diana, for instance, he stood up, glass in hand, and declared, "Here's a toast to Prince Charles and his lovely lady, Princess David!" It was then that actor Peter Ustinov was heard whispering to another guest, "He must be thinking about next weekend at Camp Diana."

TOTALLY WINGING IT

The Irish-born American stage actress Ada Rehan once played a heroine in a romantic comedy opposite a nervous young actor. During one scene she asked him a question that was crucial to the plot and then paused to wait for his answer. But the actor had forgotten his line, which was, literally, "You don't reply." Someone in the wings frantically prompted him: "You don't reply . . . You don't reply." The young man, who was at his wit's end, thought it was a critique of his performance. He exclaimed with great irritation, "Well, how the hell can I reply, when I don't know what to say?"

AND HE'S ALSO BEEN DEAD FOR CENTURIES

After Daniel Webster's death, Congressman Jerry Simpson of Kansas eulogized the great Massachusetts senator, orator, and lawyer. However, at one point he confused Daniel with Noah Webster (no relation) and praised the latter's dictionary, the first one written and published by an American. A congressman next to him whispered, "*Noah* made the dictionary," to which Simpson, his mind plunging deeper into his senior moment, whispered back, "Noah built the *Ark*!"

WE TRIED TO GET THE PRESIDENT, BUT HE WAS BUSY

New York congressman Clarence E. Hancock was one of several speakers at a meeting of a women's club in his district. Hancock, who served in the House for twenty years, was introduced by the club's chairwoman: "Members, this is our last meeting of the year," she began, "and we have enjoyed a splendid program. Our speakers have been both entertaining and instructive. But today we have something quite different. I present Congressman Hancock."

THE FIRST VIRTUE IS NOT BEING ABLE TO REMEMBER VIRTUES

On his eightieth birthday, writer Somerset Maugham spoke at a dinner held in his honor in London. "There are many virtues in growing old," he began, but then stopped and stared down at the table. The pause grew into a long, awkward silence. Maugham looked absently around the room, shifting from foot to foot, glancing helplessly at his notes. Finally, he cleared his throat and explained, "I'm just trying to think what they are."

WHAT A COINCIDENCE! IT HAS THE SAME NAME AS I DO!

While working with certain equations, the great mathematician David Hilbert suggested a revolutionary idea that led to the development of a new kind of geometry. It involved multidimensional spaces that came to be known as "Hilbert spaces." Some time later, Hilbert attended a conference with fellow mathematician Richard Courant. Several papers presented there referred to *this* or *that* Hilbert space. After one such presentation, a genuinely puzzled Hilbert turned to his colleague and asked, "Richard, exactly what is a Hilbert space?"

HONEY, I'M STILL HAPPY TO GIVE
YOU MY AUTOGRAPH

Doris Day was walking down a Beverly Hills street one day when a man stopped her. Assuming he was a fan, Day said hello and started to move on.

"Don't you remember me?" the man called after her. "No," the actress replied. "Should I?" "Well, you didn't have *that* many husbands," replied her second husband, saxophonist George Weidler.

WHEN CUSTOMERS
REALLY CLEANED UP

In 1992, as a promotional gimmick, the British division of the Hoover vacuum cleaner company offered two free, round-trip airline tickets from London to other European cities. All you had to do in order to qualify was buy $150 worth of Hoover products. If you bought $375 worth, you got two free round-trip tickets to New York or Orlando. Apparently people at the company had forgotten to do the math. More than 20,000 customers got free tickets before Hoover ended the promotional campaign, having lost $50 million.

HINDI, ON THE OTHER HAND, WOULD HAVE BEEN A BREEZE

Mark Boyle decided he would walk from Bristol, England, to Mahatma Gandhi's birthplace in western India without carrying any money—to demonstrate the importance of humility and the superficiality of wealth. He figured it would take him two-and-a-half years to reach India, starting with a trek to the English coast and a ferry to Calais, France, in early 2008. But Calais was as far as he got. He explained later that it was just too hard to communicate. It seems he didn't remember that the French spoke a foreign language—namely, French—which he did not.

SPACE, THE FINAL FRONTIER OF MEMORY LAPSES—MISSION 2

On July 22, 1962, the *Mariner 1* space probe was launched from Cape Canaveral. Its scientific mission: to reach Venus after 100 days in space, go into orbit, and then send back valuable data. But four minutes after the launch, the $18 million rocket veered dangerously off course and had to be destroyed by remote control. The cause? Someone had forgotten to put one symbol into the computer's program.

CAUTION: THIS ICE MAY BE COLD

The business world must have a pretty good idea of just how absentminded some people can be if the explicit warnings they put on packages are any indication. For example, on a package of Hormel pepperoni, there's "Do not eat packet," and for a Rowenta iron, there's "Do not iron clothes on body." And then there are these other classics: "Do not take if allergic

to Zantac" on a box of Zantac 75, and
"Do not drive a car or operate machinery,"
a warning to all those forgetful kids taking
Boots Children's cough medicine.

UNTIL TOTAL AMNESIA DO US PART

In 1920 Albert Muldoon agreed to be the
best man for his friend Christopher at a
marriage ceremony in Kileter, a village in
Northern Ireland. But having forgotten where
to stand during the ceremony, he wound up
on the wrong side of the groom. The priest,
never having laid eyes on the happy couple,
addressed Muldoon during the service
instead of Christopher. Muldoon, by now
thoroughly muddled, dutifully answered the
priest's questions while Christopher suffered
his own senior moment, having forgotten
how the ceremony was supposed to go. It
was only when Muldoon was poised to sign
his name in the registry under the heading
of "Groom" that the bride realized she was
about to marry the wrong man.

SAY YOU'LL CALL BACK—
WE'RE IN THE MIDDLE OF A PLAY

Actor A. E. Matthews's memory
deserted him at the most inopportune
times. Matthews once appeared in a play
involving a telephone call that was critical
to the plot—a call that Matthews was
supposed to answer. But when the phone
rang on cue and Matthews picked up the
receiver, his mind went blank. Desperate,
he turned to the other actor on stage and
said, "It's for you."

MAYBE WE CAN SELL IT AS
A VERY LARGE BATH TOY

As the old proverb says, measure twice
and cut once—or in other words,
make sure your measurements are correct
if you don't want to waste time, material,
and money. The producers of the film *Raise
the Titanic* either never learned the adage
or forgot it completely. They built an exact
scale fifty-five-foot model of the doomed

ship for $350,000 (for a few special effects shots), but they didn't bother to check if the model would fit into the studio's water tank. So they were forced to build a larger tank at the cost of $6 million, which was only $1 million less than the entire gross of the doomed film.

AND TO THINK I'M *STILL* GOING TO THE HALL OF FAME

In the early 1900s, pitcher Rube Waddell of the Philadelphia Athletics, perhaps the most eccentric baseball player in history, often wandered off between innings when he was supposed to be in the dugout. Once, after a frantic search, teammates found him shooting marbles with some local kids behind the ballpark; another time, he left to chase a fire truck. He sometimes arrived just a few minutes before game time, made his way through the stands, and jumped onto the field, tearing off his clothes as he approached the clubhouse to change into his uniform.

GET SHAKESPEARE—
WE NEED A REWRITE!

For a Columbia Pictures film about big business, a screenwriter needed an important speech for the CEO to deliver to his board of directors. So he picked one that Spartacus, the Roman slave turned rebel leader, had made to his followers. "What the hell is this?" said Columbia head Harry Cohen when he read the script. The screenwriter explained where the speech came from, but Cohen wasn't buying it. "I don't want any of that crap," he said impatiently. "I want a speech that everyone in the audience will recognize immediately." "You mean like Hamlet's soliloquy?" asked the screenwriter. "No! No!" yelled Cohen, who was known for his terrible temper and his equally bad memory. "I mean something like 'To be or not to be!'"

I BET WILSON WOULD HAVE REMEMBERED

President William Howard Taft had an inconvenient problem for a politician: He couldn't remember names—not even the names of his staunchest supporters. At one rally, when Taft was running for re-election against Woodrow Wilson, he confessed to a big contributor, "My advisers tell me I *ought* to remember you, but bless my soul, I cannot recall you at all!" (Needless to say, the contributor contributed nothing after that.)

INDELIBLY YOURS

James J. Sylvester, a professor at Johns Hopkins University in the 19th century, was notoriously absentminded. One afternoon, just as one of his students was going out for a walk, Sylvester handed him an ink bottle and asked him to drop it in the letterbox, since he was very anxious to have an immediate reply.

AND, FURTHERMORE,
ONCE YOU TELL ME,
I'LL DISAGREE WITH YOU EVEN MORE!

The 19th-century English novelist Anthony Trollope worked for the post office most of his life. It was his habit of waking very early and writing at great speed before leaving for the office that may have brought on this senior moment: At a staff meeting one day, Trollope snapped at a colleague who had spoken before him, "I disagree with you entirely! What was it you said?"

EXCEPT FOR THAT, I THINK
WE'RE IN PRETTY GOOD SHAPE

In Cuba during the Spanish-American War, U.S. soldiers charging up San Juan Hill were quickly confronted with barbed wire, a typical first line of defense. Unfortunately, no one had remembered to bring wire cutters. Artillery support, which is also a given in an infantry assault, had been forgotten as well.

WHOSE SIDE ARE YOU ON?

Officials of Teamsters Local 988 of Houston, Texas, must have forgotten they were running a union when they built a new meeting hall using nonunion labor. They then compounded their gaffe by responding to a reporter's request for an on-the-record explanation with the statement, "Union workers cost too much."

FIRST LADY OF FORGETFULNESS

While in the White House, John F. Kennedy found a note with the reminder "Department store—$40,000." Immediately recognizing his wife's handwriting, and familiar with Jackie's shopaholic ways, he confronted her. "What the hell is this?" he demanded. She looked at the note, thought for a moment, and said, "I don't remember."

PLEASE HAVE THAT MAN
REMOVED AT ONCE

The great conductor Arturo Toscanini would often sing along with the orchestra during rehearsals. But sometimes he would forget what he was doing. Once, during a dress rehearsal, his voice was so loud that it could be heard above the instruments. Suddenly he stopped the orchestra. "For the love of God," he snapped, "who's singing here?"

ON THE OTHER HAND,
I'LL BE BORED OUT OF MY MIND

One Sunday George Salmon, a 19th-century professor of divinity at Trinity College, Dublin, absentmindedly brought to church the same sermon he had preached the year before. Unable to think of anything else to do, he pressed on, reading from the text. He later explained his reasoning this way: that half the congregation had surely not been in church back then, so it was new to them; that one quarter *had* heard the sermon, but was just as absentminded as he was, and no doubt had forgotten it altogether; and that the final quarter of the congregation would be happy to hear it again regardless.

DAMN! I KNEW I SHOULDN'T HAVE MISSED THE LAST SIX REHEARSALS

At an American performance of Verdi's opera *Ernani* in 1847, the tenor, playing a bandit of noble descent, made a grand entrance from stage left only to find that the rest of the cast was facing stage right, waiting for him to appear. Next, he tried to pull out his sword for his big aria, only to have it get stuck in the scabbard. When he finally got it out, he couldn't get it back in. By now completely desperate, he raced for the stage exit, only to discover that he had picked the wrong one. It was nailed shut.

ALSO, I'D FILM MYSELF
ONLY IN CLOSE-UP

One day movie mogul Cecil B. DeMille found himself directing a scene in which a cowboy was supposed to fall off his horse after a rifle shot. "No matter what happens,"  DeMille told the cameraman, "I want you to keep filming. Don't stop for anything." The scene began perfectly, but it was so realistic that a studio doctor, new to the ways of Hollywood, thought that the cowboy had actually been injured. He raced onto the set to give him first aid, ruining the rest of the shot. An enraged DeMille jumped up and ran after him, shaking his fist and cursing so vociferously that the doctor fled. When DeMille watched the rushes later, he was surprised to see the doctor dash into the scene pursued by a bald man shaking his fists and cursing. "Who in the world is that?" DeMille asked, genuinely puzzled.

"That's the studio doctor," an assistant replied. "No," DeMille said. "I meant the other man who was using such foul language." "That, sir, is you," the assistant explained. "Young man," DeMille declared, "that may appear to be me, but I assure you it is not. I never use language like that."

SHE MUST HAVE REALLY GOTTEN INTO CHARACTER

It's impressive how absentminded people can passionately deliver their convoluted answers to unexpected questions. Asked to speak about the "meaning" of her coming-of-age comedy *Clueless* (based on Jane Austen's novel *Emma*), actress Alicia Silverstone replied, "I think that *Clueless* was very deep. I think it was deep in the way it was very light. I think lightness has to come from a very deep place . . . if it's true lightness."

AND A TRUE TRIUMPH OF FORGETFULNESS!

A ctor Paul Greenwood made senior moment history when he performed on the London stage in the play *The Happiest Days of Your Life* on opening night. At the very beginning of the first scene, he was supposed to write down a note, but he couldn't find a pencil or pen in his pocket. There was dead silence in the theater as the audience waited for something to happen. When Greenwood finally recovered his power of speech, it was clear that he had completely forgotten his lines. He proceeded to make them up, although he did try to follow the general thrust of the play. In the third act, he asked the audience, "Shall I start again?" Amazed by the entire evening, they shouted back "Yes!" In its review, *The Times* of London called it "memory loss on a grand scale."

GENIUS GETS GIRL, GENIUS LOSES GIRL, GENIUS FINDS GIRL, GENIUS LOSES TICKET

In late 1930 Albert Einstein left Berlin to visit the United States. The Einstein Archive contains the following summation of a page reproduced from his travel diary: "The page depicted here describes the hectic departure of Einstein and his wife Elsa from the railway station in Berlin, 30 November 1930. First he loses his wife, finds her again, and then he loses the tickets and finds them as well. Thus began Einstein's second trip to the United States."

STAMP OUT GEOGRAPHICAL ILLITERACY

In 1999 the U.S. Postal Service printed a set of 60-cent stamps with a picture of the Grand Canyon that read "Grand Canyon, Colorado." Unfortunately, the Grand Canyon is in Arizona.

THE FOURTH ANNUAL
G. K. CHESTERTON AWARD
FOR ABSENTMINDEDNESS
GOES TO . . . G. K. CHESTERTON!

The wife of writer G. K. Chesterton grew accustomed to the breathtaking variety of her husband's senior moments. Once, when he was taking a bath, she heard him get out of the tub. After a long pause, there was a loud splash. It turned out that Chesterton had forgotten what he was doing and climbed back into the tub. When he realized his mistake, he cried out, "Damn, I've been here before!"

I'M SURE WE CAN USE THE HOLES
FOR SOMETHING

While resurfacing a road in Bath, England, a contractor accidentally paved over the steel cover of an underground fire hydrant. This made it impossible to reach the hydrant in an emergency. Consequently, a firefighter was given the important job of locating it by using a metal detector. When the device first signaled the presence of metal, the fireman dug a shallow hole in the pavement, expecting to find the cover. But strangely, it wasn't there. So he tried again and again—guided each time by the metal detector's signal. It was only after digging seven holes in the road that he remembered that his boots had steel toe caps, which had set off the detector with each step he took—again and again.

THIS SHOULD DO THE TRICK

Barry Buchstaber was standing beside a car that had two broken windows when a San Mateo County, California, deputy sheriff asked him for identification. Buchstaber absentmindedly handed him the one official-looking document he had: a copy of an arrest warrant sworn out against him for driving with a suspended license.

I FORGET WHAT THEY CALL IT
WHEN YOUR SENIOR MOMENT
LASTS A DECADE

The late rock star David Bowie once said that he could no longer remember important chunks of his life, a predicament he blamed on drugs. "I can't remember, for instance, any—*any*—of 1975!" he lamented.

I'M AFRAID WE'RE GOING TO HAVE TO
SUBTRACT YOU FROM THE TEAM, NIELS

The Danish physicist Niels Bohr, an excellent athlete in his youth, was the goalkeeper for one of the best soccer teams in Denmark in 1905. Once, while his team was playing a German club, an opposing player launched a long shot toward the Danish goal. Everyone expected Bohr to come out and grab it right away, but instead he stood gawking absentmindedly at one of the goal posts. What was it that had so captured his attention? Some mathematical calculations he had written on the post earlier in the game. The Germans scored, and Bohr never made the national team. Instead, he had to settle for a Nobel Prize.

I WAS JUST CHECKING TO SEE IF YOU REMEMBERED

Legendary talent agent and producer Leland Hayward represented top screenwriters and such high-powered stars as Katharine Hepburn, Gene Kelly, Judy Garland, Fred Astaire, and Ginger Rogers. One day Rogers complained about a script she had been sent by a certain producer. Hayward went directly to the producer's office. "How can you insult Ginger with such trash, such drivel, such rot!" he shouted. The producer yelled back, "Get out of here before I throw you out! You sold us that story!"

LET'S HEAR IT FOR THE POPE

W hen President Richard Nixon visited the Vatican, his secretary of defense, Melvin Laird, showed up smoking a huge cigar, which he was promptly told to get rid of before the pope arrived. The secretary of defense obliged, putting it in his pocket— but neglected to put it out first. Just as the pope appeared, Laird's jacket started to smoke and then caught fire. Laird frantically slapped at his pocket, prompting several other guests to join in what they mistook to be a round of applause for the pontiff.

AT LEAST HE DIDN'T ASK
WHO WON THE CIVIL WAR

A merican actor Joseph Jefferson was in the elevator of the New York Stock Exchange building when a man with a familiar face got in. He greeted Jefferson very warmly and graciously, but Jefferson couldn't place the man for the life of him. "I asked him as a sort of feeler how he happened to be in New York," Jefferson explained later to a friend, "and he answered, with a touch of surprise, that he had lived there for several years. Finally, I told him in an apologetic way that I couldn't recall his name. He looked at me for a moment and then he said very quietly that his name was Ulysses S. Grant." The friend asked Jefferson what happened next. "Why, I got out at the next floor."

I BET YOU COULDN'T TELL ONE MOUNTAIN FROM ANOTHER, EITHER

Even animals can have senior moments. Bruno, a St. Bernard rescue dog in the Alps, was famous for forgetting where he was and where he was going. Once, a search party had to be sent out to find him, which took more time than recovering the climbers he was supposed to rescue in the first place. That was the eighth time in two years that Bruno had suffered a severe memory lapse, and it brought his employment to an inglorious end.

SO THAT'S WHAT THEY WERE FOR

It was a spectacular and embarrassing senior moment. In the fall of 2015, an unmanned military surveillance blimp came loose from its mooring in Maryland and drifted over Pennsylvania for 100 miles, downing power lines and leaving tens of thousands of people without electricity. Fighter jets were sent up to track the blimp. Students were sent home after classes were canceled. The media pounced. It was a complete fiasco. And when the results of the inevitable investigation were revealed, the Pentagon admitted that there was a backup device on board that should have deflated the blimp as soon as it malfunctioned, bringing it down to the ground within two miles. But that never happened because no one had remembered to install the batteries that would have powered the "fail-safe" device.

SPACE, THE FINAL FRONTIER OF MEMORY LAPSES—MISSION 3

In 1999, NASA scientists sent the Mars Climate Orbiter 416 million miles to orbit the red planet and study its surface. Two teams were responsible for navigation. Unfortunately, one used American measurements, the other used the metric system, and both forgot to check the other's calculations. Before the spacecraft could make it into orbit, it headed straight down to the planet's surface and crashed.

WE REALLY SHOULD KEEP BETTER TRACK OF THESE THINGS

The National Park Service had an expensive senior moment when it spent $230,000 to buy a small parcel of land in Washington, D.C. It seemed like a great bargain until it was revealed two years later that the Park Service had already bought the land—in 1914.

THE UNIVERSAL GRAVITATION
OF FORGETFULNESS

The scientific genius of Sir Isaac Newton is unquestionable. Not so his memory. One day Dr. William Stukely, a scholar best known for his studies of Stonehenge and a stranger to Newton, called at Newton's house and was told by a servant that Sir Isaac was in his study and couldn't be disturbed. Stukely sat down to wait. A short time later another servant brought in Newton's dinner, a boiled chicken under a cover, and put the dish down on a table next to the visitor. When an hour had passed and Newton still hadn't appeared, the hungry Stukely ate the chicken without thinking. Finally Newton came in and apologized for having kept his visitor waiting. "Give me but leave to take my short dinner," he said, "and I shall be at your service; I am fatigued and faint." Upon removing the cover, he found only a pile of bones. Embarrassed by what he took to be yet another of his frequent lapses of memory, he put back the cover and said, "If it weren't for the proof before my eyes, I could have sworn I hadn't dined."

YOU CAN NEVER CATCH A CAB WHEN YOU NEED TO

When thinking about scientific problems, André-Marie Ampère, the absentminded French physicist, often took a piece of chalk from his pocket and wrote on the nearest convenient surface. Once, while walking in Paris, he was struck with a sudden insight about a particular problem. Seizing the moment, he began to write a series of notes and equations on the first available surface he could find—which happened to be the back of a hansom cab that was parked on the street. When the entire surface was covered, he was shocked to see his "blackboard" pull away and vanish down the street, taking with it the solution to the problem.

WITH MORE TIME,
HE COULD HAVE HAD A TRIPLE!

A veteran speechmaker, President Gerald Ford was famous for his absentminded remarks. Once he had a "double" senior moment while addressing the student body at Mesa State College in Colorado, pronounced *May-sa*. First he called it "Meesa College," and then, correcting himself, "Messa College."

HOOPS!

The Dallas Mavericks were playing the Los Angeles Lakers in game four of the National Basketball Association Western Conference semifinals. When there were just six seconds left, Dallas rookie Derek Harper pulled down the rebound of a Laker shot and began to dribble to run out the clock. It's the right strategy when your team's ahead, but unfortunately, the score was tied, a fact that somehow escaped

Harper. Neither his incredulous teammates' shouting nor 20,000 Mavericks fans' screaming prevented him from dribbling until the buzzer sounded. The game went into overtime, the Lakers won, they won the next game, too, and went on to the finals. The Dallas Mavericks—and Harper— stayed home.

AND WITH RERUNS I'D BE AS OLD AS METHUSELAH!

On *Downton Abbey*, actress Maggie Smith played the sharp-tongued Dowager Countess of Grantham. When it was announced in 2015 that the sixth season of the series would be the last, Smith was relieved. Not because she was retiring from acting, but because the series's writer/creator hadn't been keeping count of the Dowager's passing years. "I mean [my character] certainly can't keep going," said Smith. "To my knowledge, I must be 110 by now."

AT LEAST I HIT *SOMETHING*

Sport shooter Matthew Emmons had already won a gold medal in the 2004 Summer Olympics, for shooting in the prone position. When it became clear that he had a chance to win yet another gold medal in the three-position competition— only needing a mediocre score in his final shot—he calmed himself down, determined to shut out any possible distraction. He was so calm and focused, in fact, that he forgot to look at the number above the target and shot at the wrong one. He came in eighth.

THE FINE POINTS OF
SENIOR MOMENT ETIQUETTE

The British writer and actor Hesketh Pearson was in a London theater one day, waiting to speak to Sir Herbert Beerbohm Tree, an actor himself and the manager of the theater. A few seats away another man was waiting for Tree as well. When Tree finally arrived, he sat down

between them and said to both, "Consider
yourselves introduced. I only remember
one of your names, and that wouldn't be
fair to the other."

YOU KNOW, IT'S THAT AMERICAN PHILOSOPHICAL MOVEMENT CONCERNED WITH SPIRITUALITY . . .

Essayist, poet, and philosopher
Ralph Waldo Emerson
attended the funeral of his
good friend Henry Wadsworth
Longfellow in 1882, but the
absentminded Emerson couldn't
recall Longfellow's name. When he
turned to a fellow mourner, he referred to
his friend as "That gentleman," and then
added, "had a sweet, beautiful soul."
Emerson often forgot the names of
inanimate objects, as well, and had to refer
to them in a roundabout way. "The implement
that cultivates the soil" was a plow and
"the thing that strangers take away" was
an umbrella.

I THOUGHT MY STEED WAS GOING A LITTLE SLOWER THAN USUAL

When Reverend William Lisle Bowles (1762–1850) took his daily horseback ride on a toll road, he paid the gatekeeper two pence for the privilege. One day Bowles passed alone through the gate on foot, but handed the two pence to the gatekeeper anyway. The man asked him what the money was for. "For my horse, of course," replied Bowles. "But, sir, you have no horse!" exclaimed the gatekeeper. "Oh, am I walking?" asked Bowles, looking around in confusion.

I'D LOVE TO INTRODUCE YOU TO THE NEW MATHEMATICS FELLOW

When Dr. William Archibald Spooner, the famously absentminded academic administrator and lecturer at Oxford University, invited a faculty member to a tea party "to welcome our new Mathematics Fellow," the man replied, "But, sir, I *am* your new Mathematics Fellow." "Never mind," Spooner said, "come all the same."

THE JOHNSON TOUCH

In 1961 *New York Times* reporter Russell Baker was coming out of the Senate when he ran into Vice President Lyndon Johnson, who grabbed him. "You! I've been looking for you!" LBJ said, and pulled the journalist into his office. He then harangued Baker about how important Baker was to the Kennedy administration and what an insider he was. While he was talking, LBJ scribbled something on a piece of paper, called in his secretary, and handed it to her. She took it, left the room, returned a short time later, and handed the paper back to LBJ, who glanced at it, tossed it away, and then finished his monologue. Baker later learned that Johnson had written: "Who is this I'm talking to?"

AT LEAST IT WASN'T
ANOTHER TECHNICIAN

In the early days of the space program, technicians who had the essential task of cleaning a rocket's fuel tanks before a test flight suffered an embarrassing low-tech senior moment. Since even a speck of dirt could change a rocket's flight pattern with catastrophic results, the technicians climbed into the fuel tank before each launch and cleaned every square inch. But this time, when they climbed out, the instruments monitoring the tank indicated there was still some contamination. There was nothing to do but start all over again, so they opened the hatch of the tank and began to climb down. That's when they realized they had left the ladder inside.

IPSO FACTO, INCORRECTO

The 19th-century scientist, engineer, and professor Osborne Reynolds of the University of Manchester sometimes forgot he was scheduled to give a lecture. Once, after ten minutes had passed, his students, all too familiar with his absentmindedness, sent the janitor to fetch him. A few minutes later, Reynolds came tearing into the classroom. He took a textbook from the table, opened it at random, and seized upon one formula or another. He wrote the formula on the blackboard and announced it was wrong and that he would now prove his conclusion. Forgetting his students were there, he began mumbling to himself, until finally, without remembering to write down any proof at all, he triumphantly rubbed out the equation and exclaimed that it was, indeed, clearly incorrect.

HEY, THAT'S *MY* TINKER BELL

Were you missing something after your last flight—something you forgot to put your name and address on? Here's your chance to buy unclaimed items that other people forgot. Just visit the Unclaimed Baggage Center in Scottsboro, Alabama. Each day the store stocks some 7,000 items that it buys mostly from airlines and railroads. They range from suits of armor and car engines to vacuum-packed frogs and a six-foot-tall papier-mâché Tinker Bell. A veritable monument to absentmindedness.

REALLY, HE DESERVED AT LEAST A THOUSAND

In 2012, a Taliban commander was seized by American troops in Afghanistan. Not at the end of a hard-fought battle, as you might expect, but in the middle of a senior moment. The impressively muddled commander, Mohammad Ashan, who was desperately short of money, had the great

idea of collecting the reward for turning
in . . . himself. After all, who else was better
situated to cash in on his own notoriety?
Ashan walked up to a U.S. Army checkpoint
with a "wanted" poster offering a $100
reward for the capture of one Mohammad
Ashan. According to *The Washington Post*,
a soldier pointed to the photo on the poster
and asked, "Is this you?" "Yes, yes, that's
me," Ashan replied. "Can I get my reward
now?" (The answer was no.)

THIS IS GOING TO HURT
MY PRACTICE

A Greek physician named Aesclepiades,
who practiced in Rome, was so sure
of his medical skill that he swore he would
stop being a physician if he ever became
ill himself. His boast was never truly
tested, however, because while still in
good health he absentmindedly fell down
a stairway and broke his neck.

BUT HE COULD MOVE HERE
IF HE WANTED, RIGHT?

In 1962, nearly 50,000 voters in Connecticut wrote in Ted Kennedy's name as their choice for U.S. Senator. They apparently forgot that Kennedy wasn't actually running in Connecticut. He was running in Massachusetts.

AND IT'S IRON LIEGE,
BY A SENIOR MOMENT!

Jockey Willie Shoemaker would have won the 1957 Kentucky Derby but for a world-class senior moment. Coming around the final turn, his horse, Gallant Man, was in the lead and no doubt would have stayed there if the veteran jockey, who had been in hundreds of races, had not forgotten where he was on the track. He mistook the 16th pole, the last one before the finish line, for the finish line itself and stood up in the stirrups in triumph. The horse behind him, Iron Liege, passed him and won the Derby. Shoemaker, one of the greatest jockeys of all time, was suspended for 15 days for his inexplicable lapse.

SO THAT'S WHY
THE PACKAGE WAS SO BULKY

We've all had the experience of absentmindedly misaddressing a package. In 2014, NATO did this in spades when it shipped a Hellfire laser-guided missile full of highly sensitive technology to Cuba. Originally, the missile was sent to Spain for a training exercise, and afterward it was supposed to be shipped back to Florida on a military plane. But in a remarkably unfortunate senior moment, it was put on a commercial Air France flight bound for Havana instead. Luckily, the Cubans were very understanding, especially since the missile wasn't armed, and sent it back without launching it.

ACT NOW: TWO MIRACLES
FOR THE PRICE OF NONE!

When the celebrated British actress Ellen Terry was playing the blind princess Iolanthe in a play of the same name in 1880, she forgot that her character was blind—not once, but  twice. First, she put out her hand to stop her costar from stepping on a bunch of flowers that she shouldn't have been able to see. And then, making things worse, she cried out, "Look out for my lilies!" The second time, after Terry noticed that two of her fellow actors were desperately searching the floor for an amulet they dropped during a critical scene, her sight was miraculously restored for just enough time for her to stoop down, pick it up, and hand it over.

HOW WELL HE FORGETS!

Once, while on vacation, conductor Artur Rodzinski, the former director of the New York Philharmonic, was listening to the radio when he tuned in to an open-air concert shortly after it began. Fabien Sevitzky was going to conduct Shostakovich's Fifth Symphony, a specialty of Rodzinski's. As Rodzinski listened with increasing appreciation, he turned to those who were with him and marveled, "How well he sustains that line! What excellent balance!" He admitted that he had clearly underestimated Sevitzky's skill. But when the symphony ended, there was no applause, as expected, only the announcer's explanation that the outdoor concert had been rained out and, instead, the station had played a recording of the symphony—conducted by Artur Rodzinski.

DON'T GET ME
TO THE CHURCH ON TIME

When the 18th-century vicar George Harvest had dinner at his friends' homes, he had a habit of saying good-bye at the end of the evening and then, instead of going out the door, heading up his hosts' stairs. He was often discovered sleeping in the wrong house. Most impressive of all, he left the same woman waiting at the altar twice. She was the daughter of the bishop of London, which may explain why the absentminded Harvest was posted to the village of Thames Ditton for the rest of his life.

DID YOU NOTICE HOW SHABBY
HIS HOUSE WAS?

At the University of Königsberg, where mathematician David Hilbert taught in the late 19th century, it was a tradition for each new member of the faculty to make a formal call on the senior professors.

When one new colleague called on Hilbert and his wife, the younger man sat down, put his top hat on the floor, and politely started a conversation. However, Hilbert's mind was clearly elsewhere. After a while he picked up the other man's hat, put it on his head, and led his wife out of their own house, saying to her, "My dear, I think we have delayed our good colleague enough."

AND WE BROUGHT BANDAGES, TOO!

In 1960 the young Judi Dench was playing Shakespeare's Juliet at the Old Vic Theatre in London. As she tells it, she was crouching over the lifeless body of her cousin Tybalt, crying out, "Where are my father and my mother, nurse?" when her actual father, a doctor, who was in the audience with her mother and apparently seized by a senior moment, stood up and announced, "Here we are, darling, in row H!"

I DO ALL MY BEST THINKING
IN FLANNEL

Early one Sunday morning, the great 18th-century thinker Adam Smith wandered into his garden and began to ponder a deep philosophical question. Without paying any attention to where he was going, he opened his gate and began to walk along the street. He was brought to his senses only by the sound of church bells. People arriving for morning services were astonished by the sight of the eminent philosopher and economist wearing only his nightgown— twelve miles away from his home.

ALTHOUGH THE ONES
I'M USED TO PLAYING FOR
AREN'T USUALLY SO ALERT LOOKING

Walking with a friend one day in New York, Fritz Kreisler, the Vienna-born violinist and composer, passed a large fish shop. Kreisler suddenly stopped, looked at the fish, and snapped out of a

senior moment. "Heavens!" he exclaimed
to his friend. "That reminds me. I should
be playing at a concert!" The fish, arranged
in rows, mouths open and eyes staring,
had reminded him of a concert audience.

I TOLD YOU WE SHOULD HAVE JUST GRABBED SOME SNACKS

In 2009, two absentminded thieves
had the bright idea of breaking into a
Jersey City, New Jersey, grocery store to
steal its ATM. Although they got away, the
machine didn't. When the police arrived,
they found it lying in the middle of the
street just outside the store. Apparently
the robbers had put the machine in the
back of their truck but forgotten about the
electric cord that was still attached. When
they drove off, the cord got stuck in the
store door, pulling the ATM out the back
of their truck. Their total haul? Zero. The
purloined machine was still full of money.

SPACE, THE FINAL FRONTIER OF MEMORY LAPSES—MISSION 4

In 2004, a NASA probe was sent 900,000 miles from Earth to collect solar particles. With its mission accomplished, the *Genesis* spacecraft would re-enter the upper atmosphere, at which point its rapid deceleration would trigger the deployment of two parachutes. Then it would float back to terra firma. That, at least, was the plan. Instead, the capsule slammed into the Utah desert when the parachutes failed to open. It turns out the deceleration sensors failed to work, because someone had absentmindedly installed them upside down.

WELL, IF THE SHOE FITS . . .

The absentminded Russian composer Alexander Scriabin once arrived at a party wearing a pair of brand new boots. But when he returned home, he was wearing a pair of old boots instead, although he couldn't remember putting them on. More astonishingly, the boots didn't even match.

SHOULD YOU NEED
ANOTHER OPERATION,
DON'T HESITATE TO COME BACK

Two Norwegian doctors writing for the *Canadian Medical Association Journal* described the case of a young, ambitious 19th-century doctor in Norway who was finishing up a year as the assistant of a renowned surgeon. It was the custom then to have little communication with such an important man, even though they had worked side by side. As the young doctor prepared to leave his assistantship, he arranged with the head nurse for a moment to speak to the surgeon. He then thanked the great man for the time he had spent in the department and bid him goodbye. The surgeon peered over his glasses and replied, "Thank you. I hope you have fully recovered and are satisfied with the treatment you received."

AND GAVE HIM THE NAME "WHITE MAN WITH HEAD IN CLOUDS"

Thomas Nuttall, a pioneer 19th-century botanist, was known almost as much for his absentmindedness as for his brilliant field work along the Missouri River and in the Pacific Northwest. He had a great talent for wandering away from the rest of the group and getting lost, forcing his colleagues to light beacons to help him find his way back to camp. One night he didn't return at all, and a search party was sent out. But Nuttall assumed the searchers were Indians and ran away, getting even more lost. His annoyed colleagues pursued him for three days, until he accidentally wandered back into camp. Another time Nuttall got so lost, he wandered around for hours until he could walk no more and lay down in exhaustion. Fortunately a passing Indian took pity on him, brought him three miles to the nearest river, and paddled him home in a canoe.

AND YOU MIGHT ADD MY MEMORY
TO THAT LIST, TOO

When 19th-century Anglican archbishop Richard Chenevix Trench retired from the post of Dean of Christ Church in Dublin, he spent his last two years in London. On returning to visit his successor, Lord Plunkett, in Dublin, Trench's memory lapsed and he forgot that he was no longer the host, remarking to his wife during dinner, "I'm afraid, my love, that we must put this cook down among our failures."

ON SECOND THOUGHT,
I'LL SIT DOWN AND BE ASHAMED

On Disability Day in Texas, Gib Lewis, the Speaker of the State House of Representatives from 1983 to 1992, called out to a group of people in wheelchairs, "And now, will y'all stand and be recognized?"

TENNYSON, ANYONE?

One day the Reverend George Clayton Tennyson, the father of the great poet Alfred, Lord Tennyson, went to visit a parishioner. When a servant answered the door and asked who was calling, Tennyson's mind went blank, and he found to his surprise that, for a few moments, at least, he couldn't summon up his own name. Distraught, he started to walk away, until a village tradesman smiled at him and said, "Good day to you, Dr. Tennyson." "By God, my man," Tennyson replied excitedly, "you're right!"

A GRAVE IS A TERRIBLE THING TO WASTE

An absentminded doctor had just pronounced a man dead in Pecaya, Venezuela, but when the first shovelfuls of earth were being flung into the man's grave, the unconscious victim, who had suffered a nonfatal heart attack, came to, pushed open the lid of his coffin, and scrambled out of the hole, screaming and cursing. Sadly, his mother-in-law, who was standing by the side of the grave, promptly dropped dead of shock. She was then buried in the grave intended for her son-in-law, after other doctors made sure she was really, really dead.

AT LEAST I DIDN'T LEAVE
MY WALLET IN THE BACKSEAT

Even the celebrated cellist Yo-Yo Ma, who has memorized hundreds of musical compositions, has been laid low by senior moments, none more nearly disastrous than when he left his $2.5 million cello in a taxi after a Carnegie Hall concert. When it was recovered, he was asked how he could have forgotten something so precious. "Practice," he replied.

YOUR NOSE LOOKS
ESPECIALLY UNFAMILIAR

The Reverend William Spooner, the dean of New College at Oxford University starting in 1876 and namesake of "spoonerisms," once ran into an old acquaintance. "Good evening, Dr. Spooner," the man said. "I don't suppose you remember me." Spooner looked at him for a moment and replied, "On the contrary, I remember your name perfectly, but I've completely forgotten your face."

THANK GOODNESS THEY DON'T HAVE
LONG-RANGE MISSILES

In 2009, a BBC Radio Five newsreader mistakenly announced that an illegal underground nuclear test had been carried out by, of all places, North Yorkshire, England, instead of the real culprit, North Korea. Further compounding the senior moment, the newsreader added, "There has been widespread condemnation of North

Yorkshire's decision . . . The UN secretary, Ban Ki-Moon, says he is deeply worried." A spokesman for BBC Radio Five tried to make the best of a bad situation when he pointed out that just as there were tensions between North and South Korea, there was "the occasional tension between North and South Yorkshire."

WHY, WE COULD USE ONE JUST LIKE IT IN OUR NEW FILM!

While discussing the score of a new MGM film, Samuel Goldwyn, a great admirer of Cole Porter, told everyone working on the production that they needed a song like "Night and Day." Soon thereafter, the studio chief visited the home of one of his associates, where the song was playing on the phonograph. "What tune is that?" asked Goldwyn.

AND A PARTRIDGE IN A PEAR TREE MIGHT BE NICE, TOO

In 1948, when the host of a radio station in Washington, D.C., asked foreign ambassadors what they would like for Christmas, one of them forgot the first rule of diplomacy: Always stay on message. The French ambassador remembered. He said gravely, "Peace throughout the world." The Russian ambassador remembered, too, and gave a very Soviet answer. He said, "Freedom for all people enslaved by imperialism." But the British ambassador, Sir Oliver Franks, must have thought he was at home and off duty. "Well, it's very kind of you to ask," he said. "I'd quite like a box of crystallized fruit."

AND YOUR BUTTOCKS WILL SOON BE DEAD!

American actor Osgood Perkins was appearing in a play in which he had to stab another actor with a knife. One day, however, the prop man forgot to put the weapon on the table. Thinking fast to spare both the absentminded prop man and himself embarrassment, Perkins kicked the other actor in the rear. As the man fell down, Perkins announced to the audience, "Fortunately, the toe of my boot was poisoned!"

FORTUNATELY, THE X-RAY OF THE SCREWDRIVER WAS NEGATIVE

In Cannes, France, doctors were stunned when an X-ray of a man who was having headaches revealed a 7-inch-long screwdriver in his head! What kind of terrible accident could account for such a thing? How could the patient have survived? It was soon discovered, however, that the screwdriver was not in the man's head after all, but in the X-ray machine. A technician had left it there and forgotten all about it.

THE FIFTH ANNUAL G. K. CHESTERTON AWARD FOR ABSENTMINDEDNESS GOES TO . . . G. K. CHESTERTON!

On one occasion, writer G. K. Chesterton was heading off to make a speech when he suffered a senior moment sufficient to force him off the train to telegraph his wife: "Am in Market Harborough. Where ought I be?" She wired back: "Home."

SO THERE *IS* SUCH A THING AS BAD PUBLICITY

When the state of Rhode Island came up with a new slogan in 2016 to boost tourism, the best it could do was "Rhode Island: Cooler and Warmer." It confused everyone, and became the subject of countless jokes on social media ("Dumb and Dumber," anyone?). But then came the video that accompanied the $5 million publicity campaign. Absentminded (but highly paid) marketers included a scene that was shot not in Rhode Island, but in Iceland, and featured restaurants located in Massachusetts, Rhode Island's nearest and fiercest competitor for tourist dollars.

IF I KNEW WHO YOU WERE, THAT WOULD INDICATE THAT I HAD REASON TO REMEMBER YOU

When Winston Churchill was asked, "Remember me?" by someone who escaped his memory, he would reply, "Why should I?"

NOT YOU, OF COURSE. I MEAN THAT OTHER TERRIBLE WOMAN

When Sir John Gielgud told Elizabeth Taylor that Richard Burton's acting had gone downhill "since he married that terrible woman," he clearly had forgotten that the woman Burton had married was Taylor herself.

UH-OH

New York wine merchant William Sokolin was entrusted with selling a bottle of Chateau Margaux 1787 that once had belonged to Thomas Jefferson. At auction, where Sokolin set a minimum price of $500,000 on behalf of an anonymous customer, no bidder would meet his price. Afterward, he had the unfortunate idea of taking it along to dinner at the Four Seasons restaurant. As he was getting ready to leave, an absentminded waiter carrying a coffee tray suffered a physical senior moment. To the horror of everyone nearby, he bumped into the bottle and broke it, spilling the precious contents across the floor. (Although the bottle was insured, it was for less than half of Sokolin's asking price.)

DO AS I SAY, NOT AS I DON'T SAY

One day Benjamin Jowett, the dean of Balliol College at Oxford University, took a long walk with a student. In the beginning of their walk, the undergraduate made various efforts at starting up a conversation, but the absentminded Jowett was lost in his own thoughts. In fact, he didn't speak to the student at all, only occasionally murmuring to himself before lapsing again into silence. Yet at the end of the walk Jowett turned to the hapless student and advised him in no uncertain terms, "You must cultivate the art of conversation. Good morning!"

SEE? THIS PROVES MY POINT

Dallas City Council member Roland Tucker was known as a strong advocate of crime prevention. He even researched making it illegal for people to leave their keys in unattended cars. Naturally, he himself soon left his car keys in the ignition, not to mention leaving his research on preventing crime on the seat. The car was then stolen.

AND AMNESIA IS THE LANGUAGE
OF THE ABSENTMINDED

The writer and radio personality Nigel Rees once asked a guest on the BBC Radio program *Quote . . . Unquote* the following question: "Who said, 'Violence is the repartee of the illiterate?'" The guest, journalist and author Alan Brien, searched his memory. "I don't think I've heard it before," he said. "Modernish? It can't be very old. Bernard Shaw would be too good for it. Perhaps it's Chesterton. Is it?" No, the quote was from Brien himself.

REHNQUIST? WHO'S REHNQUIST?

Richard Nixon could never remember the name of his assistant attorney general, William Rehnquist. A month after they were introduced, Nixon was calling him "Renchburg." A few weeks before nominating him to the Supreme Court, Nixon still couldn't get it right and was referring to him as "Bill Rensler."

AND I MIGHT EVEN REMEMBER
TO PAY THE FARE

Max Schödl, the Austrian still-life painter, once hailed a cab in Vienna. When the driver asked, "Where to?" Schödl thought it over for a while and replied, "Number six," which is all he could remember, at least for the time being. "I'll tell you the street later on," he told the confused driver.

SADLY, THE 10-POUND NOTES
WERE A TRIFLE OVERCOOKED

It was a very busy New Year's Eve at the New House Hotel in Wales, and chef Albert Grabham chose the safest place he could think of to temporarily put the restaurant's cash and charge slips: the oven. Who would look there? Apparently no one—not even Grabham. The next morning, in preparation for New Year's lunch, he lit the oven with the money still inside.

BUT I'LL TELL YOU ONE THING: THE PERSON WHO WROTE IT KNEW WHAT HE WAS DOING

It has long been known that the use of drugs and alcohol makes it harder to remember what happened under the influence. Even so, Sir Walter Scott seems to have experienced an extraordinary memory lapse while he was addicted to laudanum, an opium-based painkiller. In 1819 when Scott read the proofs of his just-completed novel, *The Bride of Lammermoor*, he confessed that he didn't recognize a single character, incident, or conversation in the entire work.

WHO DOESN'T PREFER A TIDY NUMBER?

The mathematical constant pi, represented by the symbol π, is the ratio of the circumference of a circle to its diameter. It's an infinite decimal but is commonly approximated to 3.14 or

3.14159. You can't get through school without learning it in order to solve simple mathematical problems. Nevertheless, in 1897 the members of the Indiana house of representatives suffered a collective memory lapse when, without explanation, they passed a bill declaring that the value of pi was 3.2. This would have ensured that mathematical and engineering calculations throughout the state would go terribly wrong, had not sharper memories in the state senate prevailed.

IT WAS THE "WHATNOT" THAT REALLY BROKE THE BUDGET

President Dwight D. Eisenhower created the department known as H.E.W. (Health, Education, and Welfare) in 1953, but he couldn't seem to remember what the letters stood for. He kept calling it "Health, Welfare, and Whatnot."

BEETHOVEN'S FILTH

Beethoven often forgot to keep fires going in his room in the dead of winter. He never remembered to have his windows washed or change his shirts unless someone reminded him. Once, a local policeman, convinced that the great composer was a tramp because Beethoven hadn't remembered to put on fresh clothes for days, threw him in jail.

THE SIXTH ANNUAL G. K. CHESTERTON AWARD FOR ABSENTMINDEDNESS GOES TO . . . G. K. CHESTERTON!

Chesterton once wrote to a friend: "On rising this morning, I carefully washed my boots in hot water and blackened my face, poured coffee on my sardines, and put my hat on the fire to boil. These activities will give you some idea of my state of mind. . . ."

NEXT TIME, HOW ABOUT WE
JUST TAP HER ANKLE WITH A STICK?

In the early days of BBC television, Jasmine Bligh was one of the network's first announcers. The floor managers had decided to cue her by activating a small electrical device tied around her ankle. This device was supposed to deliver a barely perceptible jolt so she would know when to start speaking. In what has to be considered one of the more potentially fatal senior moments in history, the management forgot to test the setup in advance. The first time it was used, the director in the control room called out "Cue, Jasmine," a button was pushed, and Bligh cried out, "*AAAAARRGH!* And good evening."

WHAT A CHEAPSKATE!

To impress a woman on a date, entertainer Harry Richman sometimes tipped a waiter fifty dollars after being handed the menu. Once, Richman asked the head waiter at the deluxe Stork Club, "What's the biggest tip you've ever  received?" "A hundred dollars," the waiter told him. So Richman gave the man two hundred dollars. "Now tell me," Richman asked, "who gave you the hundred?" "You did, Mr. Richman," the waiter replied.

AND HERE'S A PHOTO OF ME BEATING HIM UP

In the summer of 2012, Michael Ruse of Hampshire, England, forgot the cardinal rule of Internet postings: When in doubt, don't post. On trial for assault, he thought his defense was going so well that he bragged on Facebook, "I think I'm going to get away with it!" When the incriminating post fell into the hands of the prosecution, his fate was sealed. After sentencing Rouse to forty-six weeks in prison, the judge pointed out that, essentially, Rouse had fully confessed—just not in court, where he probably would have received a lighter sentence.

YET SOMEHOW SHE HAS NO TROUBLE READING ROYALTY STATEMENTS

According to the husband of author Anne Rivers Siddons, when she is preparing to begin work on a new book she becomes so preoccupied that she sometimes walks into walls. Once she put a carton of orange juice out their back door and their kitten in the refrigerator.

NUMBER 16: LEAVE LIST IN CAR
SO POLICE CAN CATCH US

Two escaped prisoners from Marble Valley, Vermont, were forced to abandon a stolen car when a police officer approached them. Inside was a very helpful list the forgetful fugitives had written to help them remember what to do: "Drive to Maine, get safer place to stay, buy guns, get Marie, get car—Dartmouth, do robbery, go to New York." The prisoners were later picked up in Manhattan getting off a Maine-to-New York bus.

HOME IS WHERE
THE SHORT-TERM MEMORY IS

One afternoon, 50-year-old Jermund Skogstad was busy moving into his new apartment in Oslo, Norway, when he decided to grab some lunch. But after he finished eating at a café some distance away, he reached into his pocket and realized he had forgotten his wallet, which

contained not only his money but also his
new address—an address he couldn't
remember, no matter how hard he tried.
In a newspaper article about Skogstad's
plight, the Norwegian said he hoped his
new landlady would read the story and
rescue him from further embarrassment.

OH, YOU MUST WANT
TO SEE MY DAUGHTER,
WHO'S JUST ABOUT YOUR AGE

The great Irish poet and
dramatist William Butler
Yeats was already 54 when his
daughter, Anne, was born.
Once, when Yeats and Anne got
off the bus that stopped in front
of their house in Dublin, Yeats
absentmindedly turned and,
not recognizing her for a moment as she
reached the gate, said hazily, "Oh, and who
is it you wish to see?"

IN PRAISE
OF THE ABSENTMINDED

Let's hope that William James had it right. One day the great psychologist and philosopher was walking down a street in Cambridge, Massachusetts, with two Harvard students when one pointed out a white-bearded man who was talking to himself. The student remarked "Whoever he is, he's the epitome of the absentminded professor." Replied James, "What you really mean is that he is present-minded somewhere else."

AT LEAST THEY SPELLED
RUSHED RIGHT

It's one thing to absentmindedly misspell a word or two that you rarely use; it's another thing to go blank when spelling words that you must have used hundreds of times. Consider the candidates for office in Charleston, West Virginia: Two Republicans spelled their party as "Repblican" and "Repucican," respectively, while four Democrats wrote either "Democart " or "Democrate." Trying to explain away the senior moments, one Republican said, "I was kind of rushed," while one of the Democrats said—you guessed it—"I was rushed."

AND FINALLY . . .

Mark Twain, as he did so often, has perhaps the final word on senior moments: "When I was younger," he said toward the end of his life, "I could remember anything, whether it had happened or not; but my faculties are decaying now and soon I shall be so I cannot remember any but the things that never happened."

BIBLIOGRAPHICAL NOTE

All the stories in this book are true (so far as anyone can remember). They were adapted from a great many sources, including books, periodicals, and websites—too many, in fact, to list here without straining my memory— but I am especially indebted to the following: *2,500 Anecdotes for All Occasions*, edited by Edmund Fuller (Crown Publishers, 1942, 1970); *Absent-minded?*, by James Reason and Klara Mycielska (Prentice-Hall, 1982); *American Literary Anecdotes*, by Robert Hendrickson (Facts on File, 1990); *Awful Moments*, by Philip Norman (Penguin Books, 1986); *Bartlett's Book of Anecdotes*, edited by Clifton Fadiman and André Bernard (Little, Brown & Co., 1985); *BBC Top Gear Epic Failures*, by Richard Porter (BBC Books, 2014); *The Big Book of Senior Moments*, by Bennett Melville (Skyhorse Publishing, 2015); *The Book of Heroic Failures*, by Stephen Pile (Ballantine, 1986); *British Literary Anecdotes*, by Robert Hendrickson (Facts on File, 1990); *Broadway Anecdotes*, by Peter Hay (Oxford University Press, 1989); *Bumper Crop*, by Bennett Cerf

(Garden City Books, 1952); *The Cannibals in the Cafeteria*, by Stephen Pile (Harper & Row, 1988); *The Cassell Dictionary of Anecdotes*, by Nigel Rees (Cassell, 1999); *Celebrities Behaving Badly*, by Carol McGiffin and Mark Leigh (Summersdale, 2009); *Congressional Anecdotes*, by Paul F. Boller (Oxford University Press, 1991); *Duh!* by Bob Fenster (Andrews McMeel, 2000); *Dumb, Dumber, Dumbest*, by John J. Kohut and Roland Sweet (Plume, 1996); *Dumb History*, by Joey Green (Plume, 2012); *The Dumbest Moments in Business History*, by Adam Horowitz and the editors of Business 2.0, compiled by Mark Athitakis and Mark Lasswell (Portfolio / Penguin Group, 2004); *Epic Fail: The Ultimate Book of Blunders*, by Mark Leigh (Ebury Publishing, 2013); *Eurekas and Euphorias*, by Walter Gratzer (Oxford University Press, 2002); *The Faber Book of Anecdotes*, edited by Clifton Fadiman (Faber, 1985); *Fortean Times: World's Weirdest News Stories*, (Dennis Publishing, 2011); *Great Government Goofs*, by Leland H. Gregory III (Dell Publishing, 1977); *Great Operatic Disasters*, by Hugh Vickers (St. Martin's Press, 1985); *The Guinness Book of Humorous Anecdotes*, by Nigel Rees (Guinness Publishing, 1994); *Hollywood Anecdotes*, by Peter Hay (Oxford University Press, 1990); *Jazz Anecdotes*, by

Bill Crow (Oxford University Press, 1991);
The Little, Brown Book of Anecdotes, edited by
Clifton Fadiman (Little, Brown & Co., 1985);
The Lives of the Great Composers, by Harold
Schonberg (W. W. Norton, 1981, revised
edition); *Lords, Ladies, and Gentlemen*, by
Clifton Daniel (Arbor House, 1984); *The
Mammoth Book of Losers*, by Karl Shaw
(Constable & Robinson, 2014); *The Mammoth
Book of Oddballs and Eccentrics*, by Karl Shaw
(Robin Publishing, Carroll & Graf, 2000);
The Mammoth Book of Weird News, by Geoff
Tibballs (Robinson, 2011); *Mathematics:
People, Problems, Results*, by Douglas M.
Campbell (Wadsworth Publishing, 1984);
Mould's Medical Anecdotes, by Richard F.
Mould (Institute of Physics Publishing,
1996); *Movie Stars Do the Dumbest Things*,
by Margaret Moser, Michael Bertin, and
Bill Crawford (Renaissance Books, 1999);
My Favorite Intermissions, by Victor Borge
(Dorset Press, 1971); *Presidential Anecdotes*,
by Paul F. Boller (Oxford University Press,
1996); *Public Speaker's Treasure Chest*, by
Herbert Prochnow (Harper & Row, 1963);
*The Real James Herriot: A Memoir of My
Father*, by James Wright (Ballantine Books,
2001); *The Return of Heroic Failures*, by
Stephen Pile (Penguin, 1989); *Rock Stars Do*

the Dumbest Things, by Margaret Moser and
Bill Crawford (Renaissance Books, 1998);
The Seven Sins of Memory, by Daniel L. Schacter
(Houghton-Mifflin, 2001); *The Speaker's and
Toastmaster's Handbook of Anecdotes*, by Jacob
Braude (Prentice-Hall, 1971); *Theatrical
Anecdotes*, by Peter Hays (Oxford University
Press, 1987); *The Ultimate Book of Heroic
Failures*, by Stephen Pile (Faber and Faber,
2011); *Uncle John's Weird, Weird World*, by The
Bathroom Readers' Institute (Portable Press,
2014); *Unusually Stupid Americans*, by
Kathryn Petras and Ross Petras (Villard, 2003);
What Were They Thinking?, by Bruce Felton
(Globe Pequot, 2003); *The Wit's Thesaurus*,
by Lance Davidson (Avon Books, 1994);
Wrong Again!, by Jane O'Boyle (Plume, 2000);
and the late, lamented Anecdotage.com.

—T. F.

ACKNOWLEDGMENTS

There are so many people to thank, but let me single out eight in particular:

The late **Peter Workman**, the founder of Workman Publishing, had the final say on virtually everything, including the decision to go ahead with the first edition.

Editor in chief **Suzie Bolotin** oversaw its creation, and guided it into print.

Design director **Paul Hanson** turned it into the perfect gift book, with the help of **Galen Smith**.

My great friend **Paul Solman** was one of the first readers of the manuscript, and offered numerous invaluable suggestions. (I think he liked it, although I no longer remember, of course.)

My dear wife, **Christy Newman**, was forced to read both editions over and over again, and never screamed once. Without her help and love, I would forget my own name.

Margot Herrera was the indispensable editor of the second edition; it's been a great pleasure working with her.

And last but not least, there's my old friend **Richard Rosen** who hired me back in 2004 to write the proposal for the first edition, and was its greatest champion. A brilliant writer/editor, he shaped it with unceasing attention to detail, great creativity, and unerring instincts (although I still think I was right about that subtitle on page 19).

Thank you all.

INDEX

PHOTO CREDITS

ABOUT THE AUTHOR

Tom Friedman is a writer, editor, and executive producer who worked for public television's preeminent producing station, WGBH Boston, for nearly 25 years. In 1996, he won a Peabody Award for the science documentary series *Odyssey of Life*. He is also the author of two books about business: *Life and Death on the Corporate Battlefield*, with Paul Solman, and *Up the Ladder*.